THEOLOGY IN PICTURES

A Commentary on Genesis
Chapters One to Eleven

THEOLOGY IN PICTURES

A Commentary on Genesis Chapters One to Eleven

GEORGE A. F. KNIGHT

The Handsel Press Limited

1981

Published by
The Handsel Press Ltd.
33 Montgomery Street, Edinburgh

ISBN 0 905312 06 6

First published 1981

Printed in Great Britain by
R. & R. Clark Ltd., Edinburgh

CONTENTS

ABBREVIATIONS

ANET	Ancient Near Eastern Texts Relating to the Old Testament, ed. by J. B. Pritchard (2nd ed.; Princeton University Press, 1955)
AV or KJV	Authorized Version of the Bible, or King James Version
LXX	The Septuagint, the Greek Version of the Old Testament
MS(S)	Manuscript(s)
MT	Massoretic Text, Biblia Hebraica, ed. Rudolf Kittel, 7th ed., 1951. The Hebrew OT
NEB	New English Bible
NT	New Testament
OT	Old Testament
RSV	Revised Standard Version
Sam. Pent.	The Samaritan Pentateuch
Targ.	Targum, Aramaic Version of the Old Testament (1) Targ. Onk. Targum Onkelos (2) Targ. Jon. Targum Jonathan (3) Targ. Ps. Jon. Targum Pseudo Jonathan (4) Jer. Targ. The Jerusalem Targum
Tor	The Torah, The Five Books of Moses; the Jewish Publication Society of America, 1962
v.	verse
vv.	verses

INTRODUCTION

Chapters one to eleven of the book of Genesis form a Prologue to the whole Bible. Consequently they may be studied separately. The subject of all eleven chapters is God. Only secondarily do they deal with the origin of the universe, the creation of man, the redemption of the universe and of man, and so on. Since therefore the chief topic is God, the writers by sheer necessity have to express themselves in picture language.

No man, we read, can see God and live. Yet Jesus taught us to 'see' by analogy. He taught us to call the Eternal Being by the name Father. Abstract terms such as atonement, reconciliation, resurrection, justification, mortification, manifestation, incarnation cannot be translated into many of the living languages of today. But then these abstract terms could not be expressed in ancient Hebrew either. For example the word 'religion' never occurs in the Old Testament. Instead of using abstractions the Old Testament prefers to give us verbs of action; these in turn necessarily require a subject to the verb. In everyday life we human beings can 'see' with the mind's eye an action taking place. This leads us to 'see' what the doer of the action is like.

These chapters, then, are about the divine Actor, who, because he does act, and is not merely the Supreme *Being*, is known throughout the rest of the Bible as the Living God. It is the task of the theologian in all ages to interpret to the human mind this human awareness that God is alive and working, and to do it in such a manner that ordinary people can grasp what he is saying. The authors of Genesis 1–11 chose to do this basic thing by means of pictures, just as Jesus chose to do it by means of parables.

It has long been noted that the anonymous writer-theologian whom scholars have named J (because he wrote in Jerusalem, and because he chose to call God Jahweh) is responsible for a lengthy narrative that runs like a silver thread, beginning with this Prologue, on through the rest of Genesis, and then into the so-called historical books. This statement, however, needs modification today. J was indeed an admirable historian. But we do him an injustice if we limit his genius to the style, or *Gattung*, used by the biblical historian. This German word is employed in scholarly analysis of the Scriptures to describe a type or variety of writing, whether it be psalm, creed, law-suit, exhortation, lament, and so also history writing. Although writing even before Homer was born, J was such a profound artist and theologian that he was clearly able to handle more than one *Gattung*. In fact, he seems to have created for the first time in human history, and in creating wholly perfected, a new genre altogether, that kind of writing by means of which ultimate reality is expressed in pictures. Thus in the Genesis Prologue he uses a distinctly different *Gattung* from that which he employs from Genesis 12 onwards. The priestly editors of the whole Pentateuch, whom we designate P for convenience, thereupon in their later period learned from J how to handle this fascinating genre. So we can confidently attribute some of the material in the Prologue which is of this nature to P.

The early chapters of Genesis, then, belong to this theological category. They do not pretend to report scientific fact; to imagine that they should do so is unrealistic and unscientific in itself. For scientific thinking is a modern phenomenon, not being more than three hundred years old. It is thus still a great hindrance to the spread of the Gospel when earnest men and women insist that 'the first chapter of Genesis conforms with science'. As every thoughtful person ought to recognize, such a statement puts the cart before the horse. For it is not our task, when we study the Scriptures, to make the Bible agree with 'Science'; rather it is the reverse. The results of our modern scientific enquiries ought instead to be scrutinized in the light of the revelation that reaches us through the Bible. The study of what we call Science is always on the move. When I was a small boy I learned as a 'fact' that there is a mysterious substance that fills all the spaces between the stars and which is known as ether. Today the astro-physicist would laugh at the very suggestion. For Science is always changing, is always on the move. It is the

Word of God that abides for ever, not this deified thing known as 'Science'. In the final analysis of course there is actually no such thing as 'Science'; rather what there is is only man thinking scientifically. And man is a very human creature, loving, hating, eating, rejoicing, as well as thinking and experimenting. It is to people who live as such, then, that the Bible speaks, not to that mere abstract notion which we have learned to call science.

In the providence of God an important coincidence occurred exactly a century ago. On the one hand, it was in the 1870s that the learned world (including the Church) was shaken by the theories of Charles Darwin and others. It seemed at that time that a choice had to be made between 'believing in science' and 'believing the Bible'. In particular, the verity of the early chapters of Genesis was at stake. On the other hand, in the very same decade, the science of archaeology offered to the learned world (and to the Church) a profound insight into the ways of thinking carried on by that ancient world out of which the book of Genesis was born. From the 1870s onward, with the aid of archaeology, we have discovered that the Babylonians, the Canaanites, the Egyptians, and other ancient 'biblical' peoples carried on their profoundest philosophizing, not by employing abstract terms, but by the use of picture language. The written Egyptian language, for example, reduces all abstract notions to picture form.

The word 'myth' came to the fore in those days a century ago, just when men were being compelled to reconsider some of their basic assumptions about the Bible. We are to note, however, that the word myth bears more than one meaning. When we say that Santa Claus is 'only a myth' we are using just one meaning of the word. This is because Santa Claus is not merely the subject of fairy-tale thinking. Santa is the pictorializing in concrete imagery of the Christmas spirit, of God's love for children, such as we learn from the story of Bethlehem. It concretizes, moreover, the reality of the expression, 'It is more blessed to give than to receive'. In the normal course of events, when a child grows older, he rejects the person of Santa Claus as a 'myth'. On the other hand he has learned from the myth a great deal about the meaning of love and generosity and kindness. What has happened is that the myth has become for him a vehicle to reveal a basic reality. The myth in itself is not that reality. (See J. Neusner, *Understanding Jewish Thought*, 1973, p. 6.) The actual myth can be and is rejected. But the reality it conveyed is retained.

The nations of the Near East in the period before 500 B.C. made effective use of myth. The *Enumah Elish* (meaning 'When on high . . .') of Babylon goes back to at least the First Babylonian Dynasty, about 1830–1530 B.C., thus long predating the sources of Genesis. This extended myth was first published in English by George Smith in 1876 under the title of *The Babylonian Account of Genesis*. The story deals with the struggle between order and chaos (in themselves abstract notions), represented in the final victory of Marduk the creator god over the powers of chaos and death. In the story we hear of Apsu, the primordial father, who is the abyss of fresh water (our word abyss comes from Apsu), and of Tiamat the primordial mother, who is the salt sea. The gods are born through the union of the two waters, from out of the original chaos. Such then was the background of thought, the 'scientific climate' that Abraham absorbed as a boy at school.

In Genesis, however, we meet with the unique nature of the biblical awareness, as against that of the ancient Near East. Israel was the only people of the ancient world that ever successfully de-mythed the myth. It was actually not possible for Israel to think in a manner different from her neighbours, for she was necessarily the child of her cultural period. She too obviously wondered about the origin of the earth, the meaning of human life, the reality that man is subject to frustration and death. Consequently she wondered about these basic issues, not in philosophical, psychological, cosmological, or any other modern terms, but quite naturally in terms of myth. But here, under God, Israel, as we have said, did a unique thing. In the Genesis stories we find no mention of gods and goddesses, no reference to the a-moral acts and selfish, lustful planning that we come across in any of the ancient myths of the Near East. But the pictorial thinking of ancient man is still there, though not his philosophy, not his science, not the psychological apotheosis of divine beings that represented in living divine-human form the moods of mere man, such as the Greek genius produced. In Genesis we meet with the one reality only – God. God is not explained nor is he philosophized about. He is not man writ large in the heavens. He is just – God. But he is the living God. He acts. He creates. He creates the earth and man upon the earth, so that the earth, and man, are seen to be totally other than God.

Consequently the story is told pictorially. The shape of the Babylonian myth remains, but without the appearance of any warring deities. There is still to be found the separation of heaven and earth. There is still the seven-day framework of thought through which man, Babylonian man, understood that the growth and development of a human being takes place. But these things are not the reality in themselves; they are only the culturally-conditioned modes of thought that Israel must needs use to express her mind.

Yet this story we are about to read is not *her* mind at all. These early chapters of Genesis are not to be equated with the Law of Moses on which Jesus later on passed judgment and to which he could even add his own word of interpretation. The early chapters of Genesis are not included amongst the Prophets, some of whose words Jesus could reject outright, as, for example, when he ostentatiously rolled up the scroll from which he was reading in the Synagogue before he reached the words of Isa. 61: 2b: 'and the day of vengeance of our God'. Jesus makes no criticism, however, of the early chapters of Genesis. It is evident that he regarded them as nothing less than Revelation. So now we in our turn give thanks to God that this revelation is given to us in picture language. For picture language alone can convey reality despite the passage of time and the many changes of culture through which the world has passed, intact. Moreover, a study of these chapters becomes an exciting theological exercise. For in them we are presented with the basic structure of the theology of both the Old and the New Testaments. Bennett, in the Century Bible, expresses this truth from another angle: 'The narratives of Genesis bear much the same relation to dogmatic theology that a landscape by Turner does to an ordnance map'.

When an author's name occurs in the following commentary, without reference to chapter and verse (as 'Bennett' above), it is to be understood that he is the author of a Commentary on Genesis, and that the reference is to the verse which is under discussion.

CHAPTER 1

THE PROLOGUE TO THE PROLOGUE

―――――

1–5   *The Prologue to the Prologue.* The phrase 'When God began to create the heavens and the earth', as the footnote in the RSV puts it, embodies a translation that is an important departure from the well-known words of the AV, 'In the beginning God created'. The RSV offers a translation that is both more accurate and more theologically sound. The Deist emphasis in the thought of the Church in eighteenth-century England suggested that once God had set the universe in motion, he then retired and left the earth to spin on its own. Such a view, however, contradicts the thought of the OT. The section Isaiah 40–55, which issues from the dark period of the Babylonian exile, keeps reiterating the statement that God creates. The form of the word is a verb, an active participle to be exact; it is not a noun. God is he who 'keeps on creating', Isa. 40: 28; 43: 15, without growing weary in so doing, and who therefore has never ceased to create. This chapter one of Genesis found its present form in the same background and period as Isa. 40–55. Therefore it sounded forth Good News to that People of God who were living in despondency in a strange land. 'God is not dead,' both writers were saying. 'He can create a new situation for his exiled people.' So the first clause in the Bible can be well rendered by 'When God first began to create . . .'.

This emphasis is borne out when we recall that the noun we translate by 'beginning' means the first of a series. Again, the verb which we render 'create' appears only late in the literature of Israel. It is found only in the second half of Isaiah (where it occurs some twenty times), in Ezekiel, P, and some late Psalms. Originally the verb *bara* meant to 'cut out'; but by the time of the Exile we find it used with God alone as subject. The idea of creation out of nothing does not appear anywhere, however, in the canonical books of the OT. For such would be merely a human idea thought up only to satisfy our human curiosity. Genesis is first of all a book about God; and through the intermediacy of sanctified human minds it offers to humanity revelation of the divine mind, plan, and purpose. The verb *bara* therefore declares only that creative action is the prerogative of God. Man does not create; man only makes, manufactures, out of material already in existence, whether that be wood or metal, or the cells of the human brain. As Prov. 8: 22 declares, God created in order to reveal his will.

The first verse of the Bible is thus basically an invitation to man to praise God his Maker. God is the First, it seems, and so he is also the Last. This invitation, however, was not addressed in the first instance to all men , but was given to a people that was then trapped in holes and hidden in dungeons in Babylon, as Isa. 42: 22 describes the experience of exile. Thus it was that Israel came to perceive that this triumphant statement of revelation somehow or other subsumed even the reality of pain and suffering, realities that might eventuate in any period of history such as that of the Cross or of Auschwitz. These profound ideas had already been expressed in that ancient poem in Deut. 32: 39, centuries before Gen. 1 was penned.

The Bible, then, dares to speak of The Beginning. This is a thing which science cannot do, for science knows nothing of the basic realities of life. Science can only conceive of The Beginning as something finite. So, as L. Koehler says, 'The Creation in the OT does not belong to the sphere of natural science, but to the history of man'.

What God is this who is spoken of here, without introduction or any explanation? The noun *elohim* is plural. So at once he eludes our religious instincts. Men have created 'god' in their own image in all ages and cultures. At 1: 27 we are to learn that the Bible reverses all man's religious conceptions about 'god' being in man's image. Here we learn that it is not the god of our ideas who created the heavens and the earth. As this utterly other God asks of Job, at Job 38: 4, 'Were you there when I laid the foundations of the earth?' Thus there is justification for the answer that John Calvin is alleged to have given to an enquirer, who asked him what God was doing before he created the heavens and the earth. 'He was hotting up hell for those who would ask such questions', he is reported as saying.

Elohim can mean 'gods', and is so used at times elsewhere in the OT. But when it does mean this, then the verb that accompanies it is in the pural also. Here, however, it is singular. There is an early conception of the Divine Being that can be found in passages much older than this chapter. It is that God is a kind of chairman of a congress of divinities, as, for example, in Ps. 82: 1; 138: 1. But that is mere human thinking, like that to be found in the religiosity of India today. Then again the word *elohim* in its usages is not limited to the concept of masculinity. Israel's neighbours worshipped both male and female gods, both of whom were subsumed under the term *elohim*. But then our experience of sexual differentiation is merely the consequence of our being human beings. For example, the Spirit of God that we meet at v. 2 happens, by the accident of human language, to be feminine in gender. But that is only accident. Paul would be well aware of this weakness of language when he called Christ the Wisdom, *sophia* (fem.) of God.

We are to note, however, that such words as 'sky' and 'water' are both plural forms. Evidently the plural expressed the idea of unity in diversity. Water may be regarded as a drop from a cup; but it may also be thought of as the illimitable ocean. God is one, but his oneness is not limited to our mathematical concept of oneness. He is, of course, one in the sense of being unique, the one and only God, 'for all the rest are idols'. Yet at Deut. 6: 4, where we meet with Israel's basic statement of faith, 'Hear, O Israel, the Lord our God is one Lord', the word used for 'one' is not the Hebrew word for unique, *yahid*. The word there is *ehad*. We note with interest, therefore, at Gen. 2: 24, that the two separate creatures, the man and the woman whom God has made are to cleave together and become *one* flesh, *ehad*, the word used at Deut. 6: 4. The plural form of the noun *elohim* therefore leads naturally into the tripartite conception of the nature of God that we meet with in the next two verses of the text. Without such a revelation, of course, we could never hope to conceive that God is love.

The Hebrew language has no word for universe. Jeremiah attempts the idea when he speaks of *hak-kol*, the totality. Yet here we have expressed for us two realities. The one is God.

The other is God's Creation, the universe that God has brought into existence and which now exsits in its own right and utterly distinct from him who made it. The universe therefore is not in itself divine. Yet the Bible has a geocentric emphasis. It is this earth which is the focus of attention throughout, not the sun, moon, and stars. The latter are mentioned at 2: 1, as we shall see presently, almost as an afterthought. The particularism revealed here continues consistently throughout the Bible. We watch God's choice, not just of one planet, but of one nation, then of one area of soil, and then finally of one revelatory Figure. This biblical particularism is abhorrent to the religious and philosophical instincts of man.

2   God creates out of non-being. This is as difficult a notion for us to grasp as that of the square root of minus one. But it is a theological statement, not a scientific one. 'Without form and void' is *tohu* and *bohu*. We can dismiss the word *bohu* as an alliterative emphasis upon *tohu* that never occurs alone. The question is therefore what *tohu* means, for here is obviously a pictorial descriptive term to cover what is naturally inconceivable to the human mind.

Tohu may possibly be related to the following noun *tehom*, 'deep'. This noun, again, may have derived from the name of a female divinity in ancient Babylonian usage. In one early myth this Tiamat was torn in two by the male divinity to bring into being the elements of earth and sky. That, however, is mere mythology. There is no mythology in the Bible. The Hebrew mind did indeed at times use the pictorial categories of the myths of the nations around them. For example, Ps. 74: 12–17, takes this ancient myth of Tiamat and in poetic language uses it to declare that God is Lord of the primal deep in which dwell all the monsters that the mind of man can conceive. This we have discussed sufficiently in the Introduction. Gen. 1: 2 is therefore not mythology. Rather it is theology, or the truth about God expressed in picture language. The verse gives us information about the creative activity of God expressed in such a manner that even little children, such as we all are, can learn to read from God's picture-book what God himself is like.

Tohu may be translated poorly as 'chaos'. Karl Barth preferred to speak of it as 'the shadow cast by reality'. For since *being* is order in itself, then *tohu* is the negative side of God's

positive orderliness. To Jeremiah the word became meaningful
even as he gazed at the Wilderness of Judea where it lay only a
few miles south-east of Jerusalem, and where both John the
Baptist and Jesus each spent some time. A place where no birds
sang, no trees grew, where human habitation was unknown, a
place shaken by earthquakes, parched, waste and void,
Jer. 4 : 23–26. It is *out of* such waste, therefore, that God creates
order, not out of 'nothing'. As von Rad says at this point, this is
a possibility that always exists; cf. Rom. 5: 8. Therefore it is
out of that Wilderness that John emerges with his message; and
it is *out of* forty days and forty nights in the Wilderness of Judea
that Jesus' creative ministry arose, Luke 4: 1–14.

But Gen. 1: 2 describes that other notion of negation common
to the ancient world, that of a watery waste, perhaps of a hurricane blowing on an ocean that is lying in total darkness. A
horrifying prospect for seamen who used only hollowed out
logs as canoes! Only, the watery deep is not the waters of an
earthly sea. The 'deep', *tehom*, as we have noted, is related to the
Babylonian name of Tiamat. Our chapter therefore employs
the cultural thought form of its day just as we do that of ours,
and so manages to give us a theological picture of chaos that is
quite unsurpassed. It recurs in the theological story of Noah
and the Flood, in that of Jonah, where he is cast into the 'deep',
and in that of Jesus, when a storm on the Sea of Galilee
represents the chaos that was in the beginning. So it was only *out
of* that storm that creative 'peace' emerged, Mark 4: 35–41. Or
again, when God's creative peace is experienced only *out of* the
non-being of physical death, Luke 24: 36. In fact, chaos is so per-
vasive that its non-reality (!) exists even in the human breast, so
that only *out of* the chaos found there can man come alive in God.

Instead of 'the Spirit of God' *Tor* reads 'the wind of God'.
This is, of course, possible. The same double entendre is
possible in the Greek language also, as we see in John 3: 8,
where Jesus talks to Nicodemus. But since our passage began
with an emphasis upon the action of *God*, we should recognize
that this same emphasis is here also. Accordingly it is more
probable that we should read 'the spirit *of God*' than single out
the wind from amongst the elements of created matter, especially since creation has not yet taken place! God's Spirit is
clearly God's agent in the creation of order out of chaos.

The verb 'moving' is most interesting. It occurs only twice again in the OT, at Deut. 32: 11 and Jer. 23: 9. RSV translates the latter occurrence by 'all my bones shake'; but in what manner or movement we do not know. The ancient poem in Deut. is more explicit. For it paints a picture for us of the movement of the wings of a father eagle, even as he *flutters* over his babies, spreading out his wings, catching them (when they tumble in learning to fly from the nest high up on the cliff), and bearing them on his pinions. Moreover, we now know that the verb has this very meaning in the cognate language of Ugaritic. The picture therefore is of two things, (1) of action, for God is consistently known in the OT as the *living* God, and (2) of protective, creative, anxious *care*. Did Jesus have this verse in mind when he wept over Jerusalem, and spoke of his longing to gather its children together even as a hen gathers her brood under her wings, Matt. 23: 37?

This v. 2, then, bears no relationship whatsoever to any scientific explanation or description of the origin of matter. It is to be seen as a theological declaration of the living creative plan of the God who purposes, and will accomplish, the creation of ordered life out of the negation of chaos.

3 This theological declaration is now pictorialized for us in terms of the Word of God. We read that 'God said'. That is to say, in the beginning was the Word. And the Word was God. For a word begins as a thought in the mind (or in the heart, if we keep close to ancient thinking about the human anatomy); and so the word *is* the speaker himself, even as he goes through the process of thinking. Then the word emerges, so to speak, from the mouth when it is uttered by the speaker, requiring the co-operation of physical entities like the vocal chords, the tongue and the lips. Finally the word is separated from the speaker, and becomes an objective reality in its own right. The word then becomes thing, or, as we can say, it effects its task. It can become Light, or Day, or Firmament, or even Man, as we shall see, once the umbilical cord connecting it with the speaker is cut. We can pictorialize this whole operation for ourselves if we look at a comic strip in a newspaper. There we see the word emerging from a human mouth in the first frame, then being ringed around in the second so as to show that it is now a separate entity. In the third we see the effect in action of what was been said. Thus since we are talking, not in scientific terms, but about the creative purpose of God, it could well be that, if God so pleased, his Word could become, not merely thing, not merely man in general, but actually a particular man in a particular land on this particular earth. Moreover, since this Word is the Word of Almighty God, then it too must be almighty. Consequently it cannot return unto God void, but must accomplish that which he purposes, and succeed in the thing for which he sent it, Isa. 55: 11.

We might here simplify the language that we need, to know what this Word of God is and does. We should hear the phrase as ('Let be) Light'. That is to say, we are to hear only one word. Thereafter follows the corollary of 'said': ('and) light *became*'. It had to become; for when God speaks, the whole of the divine creativity is present in his Word. As Ezekiel consistently declares, God can only be true to himself. Thus God must always mean what he says, so that, if he says 'light', then light must come to be.

It would be foreign to biblical thinking to suppose at this point that the first object of God's creation was this thing called light, a physical element that may possibly pervade the whole of creation, and which is the source of the light of the sun, moon, and stars. For any such idea would be a human attempt to explain the creative purpose of God in terms of science – not forgetting that at the same time it would be a very unscientific statement! The Word of God must surely come forth from God himself. The Word *is* God himself in the first place, before it issues from God's mouth. There is no suggestion therefore of the pantheistic notion that God is one with his created universe. Such a notion is anathema to biblical thinking. Rather, 'light' here is the picture term necessary to help us understand both the creative nature of God and, to use human language again, the reality that the God of the Bible acts creatively through his Spirit and through his Word.

The Targums (various paraphrases in the Aramaic language of sections of the OT made at the end of the OT period) lay great stress on the fact that God acts through his Word. The Neofiti Codex I runs: 'The first night when the Lord was revealed above the earth to create it, the earth was void and empty and darkness was spread over the face of the abyss. And the Word (*Memra*) of the Lord was the light and it shone; and he called it the first night.' Thus some of the Targums identify the Light with the Word. And incidentally they link this verse in Genesis closely with Ex. 12 : 42, where we read that God spent a night of watching before instituting his redemptive act at the exodus. God's Light in the Targums is no less than his saving, creative activity.

Throughout the rest of the OT we find the expression used that God himself *is* Light – and the NT would add, 'and in him is no darkness at all', 1 John 1 : 5; 2 Cor. 4 : 6; 1 Peter 2 : 9; John 1 : 6–9. Light here is thus definitely a pictorial theological term and certainly not a scientific fact. We note, for example, how it is only later, at v. 6, that God creates matter by uttering the necessary Word, viz. 'let matter be', that is to say, 'Let it become through the instrumentality of the Word'.

4   The word 'good' is not to be understood in terms of morality. Rather it speaks of purpose, of the divine activity. For 'good' in Hebrew can often mean 'good for'. Thus, once God had created all things he saw that they were 'good', 1 : 25, that is to say, they were good for the plan he had in mind. We also read that God *saw*, is if he were surveying his new handywork, and was taking pleasure in what he was purposing to do with it all.

Gen. 1 is thus more truly a story of redemption than of creation; for the idea of redemption is really a way of describing re-creation. Creation here is clearly for the sake of man, made in the image of God, but for man who falls from that image. Consequently part of the plan is that man should be re-created in the likeness of God. To that end, since we have now learned that God creates out of chaos, we have already been shown the ultimate basis of man's security. This chapter, moreover, denies the human notion that the universe is a mere mechanism. We are well aware that order and security are realities that do not just *develop* out of chaos, as if they were like the genus bird which has developed gradually over the millennia out of the genus fish. Order and security necessarily imply that only a Person can create, and certainly not a blind force, cf. Ps. 139 : 7–12.

This sense of order is pictorialized by speaking of God's separating day from night, even as he has separated light from darkness. The Jewish ceremony of Havdala recalls this basic reality when the benediction is said over the light at the end of the Sabbath. For Jeremiah had regarded this act of God as a covenant he had made with man, one that God would never break under any circumstances, Jer. 33: 20–25.

God now particularizes the transcendent divine plan by reducing it to a 24-hour rhythm! Further, he *names* 12 of these hours as Day, and the other 12 he names Night. By giving the Day a name, God gives Day an identity in its own right, even as he recognizes Night to be the identification of all that militates against his comprehensive plan. Thus God has given Darkness freedom to exist, and names it as an entity necessary for his plan, even though it is inimical to it. All that belongs to the reign of Darkness, earthquakes, shifting deserts, storms, cancer, mosquitoes, are yet employed to serve the good plan that God has now begun to unfold. We are not told where darkness comes from, any more than we are told where chaos comes from. All we are assured is that, having identified it, God 'puts it in its place', so to speak; for he is Lord not only of the Day, but also of the Night, he is Ruler both of the known and of the unknown, Ps. 139: 12. The significance of this becomes a basic theme of those prophets and Psalmists who later ruminate on the meaning of this Prologue that we have been considering here: Ps. 29: 10; 74: 13–15; 89: 10; 93: 3–4; 104: 5–9; Isa. 51: 9; Job. 26: 10–14. The distinction between Light and Darkness came into Israel's consciousness apparently at that time when God 'made a distinction' between Egypt and Israel, Ex. 11: 7. It was as if the Word of God had acted as the sword of judgment, dividing this from that. The night of the Passover was a unique moment in the life, not just of Israel, but of God himself, for when Day broke Israel had been reborn as the redeemed People of God, Ex. 12: 42; 13: 3.

Our human life too is regulated by those 24-hour intervals. No matter how dark the night may be, no matter what black cloud should settle on the tired and weary spirit of man, even as evening turns to night, the beauty of each fresh new day beckons and speaks to him of the ever new-creating plan of God, one that is always *good for* him, in that even Darkness is part of what is positively good. Thus we are not meant to raise the question that modern man is inclined to do, as to the length

of time that 'one day' should cover. We are not even to compromise with science by quoting the words of the Psalmist:
'For a thousand years in thy sight are but as yesterday when it is
past' – for the Psalm too is speaking in poetic figures. Yet, to
speak scientifically for just one moment, we are being driven
today to the logical conclusion that the great ages of the earth,
the millennia that bridge the gap between the Palaeozoic Age
and the Mesozoic Age, and so on, are really a non-event. For
time has no meaning in itself if there is no person present in it to
experience the event.

God's Creative Work of Love, 1 : 6–2 : 3

6–8   God creates matter through his Word: 'And God
said, "Let there be . . ." '. The concept of the Word thus pre-
serves the biblical God from being supposed to create by means
of emanations from himself. This was a basic notion in the
Manichaeism which the early Church had to face, and which
the Church today must anwser as it meets with the impact of
the thought of India.

The ancient pre-biblical myths taught that the god tore the
goddess of chaos in two to create the sky and the earth. In this
verse here we very naturally find the same cultural background,
yet showing none of the bloody-mindedness that lay at the basis
of Babylonian thought. God, it seems, does not need to use his
hands. Rather it is by divine Fiat that the watery waste of chaos
is sundered. A space, the 'firmament' is left between the waters
above the chaos and the waters below it. 'And it was so.' Of
course it was. Because the Word of God *is* Almighty God himself, in action, Ps. 33 : 9. The Word does not merely have 'an
effect'; it is itself Work. 'And God called the space "the skies" ',
thus giving them also an identity as existing in reality. This day's
work was thus completed by a divine decision. For God plans
each day in such a way that what he is now completing will
work in harmony with what he has already made, and with
what he will make tomorrow.

As we saw, heaven is really the skies. For heaven is not a
supernatural 'place'. The heavens *and* the earth are all part of
God's creation, and none of it is divine. In the OT heaven has
no theological significance, nor is it the abode of God its
Creator. For God, to use the picture language that alone can

convey reality, sits *above* the heavens, utterly other than the creation he has brought into being. So there is no such thing in the OT as the realm of the supernatural. In fact that word never occurs in the Bible. There are only two realities known in revelation. First, there is God; and then second, and utterly other than God, there is the natural creation. Long before Gen. 1 was penned Israel had incorporated into her Law a refusal to allow any trafficking with a non-existent supernatural world where the souls of men might possibly continue to exist beyond the sphere of the grace of God, Deut. 18: 10–12.

The word 'firmament' comes from a root meaning 'to hammer into shape'; and so its use once again localizes the area of God's acts of grace of which we are to hear so much. And since the translation should be 'and let it go on dividing . . .', we are presented, once again in picture terms, with the realization that God's gracious plan is to continue indefinitely. Heaven, then, is to be the upper protective limit of created order, Job 38: 8–11.

The evening comes first, for the evening marks the completion of the day's toil. It is only *after* toil that man may look for the morning. So this is the divinely ordained rhythm of life on earth, Ps. 121: 8; John 9: 4. The processes of nature thus perform a service to God. Since a liturgy is an order of service, then, as Richardson expresses it, Gen. 1, like Job 38: 7, is a Te Deum addressed to God.

9–13 Now God's Word concentrates on what lies between the waters above the 'space' and the waters of the abyss below it. These waters God holds back by bars and doors, Job 38: 10; cf. Ex. 20: 4. What wetness remains God makes into Seas, out of which now emerges the dry land. This too *had* to happen: 'it was so'. Finally God established the identity in reality of both Earth and Seas by naming them in turn, and once again God saw that both of them were good *for* his plan. But before we learn what the end-product of the plan is to be, we hear next about the creation of vegetation. Life evidently arises spontaneously from the elements of earth and water.

At this point, therefore, we must note that God, having created nature, now hands over autonomy to it. It is no longer God who creates the generations of plants, it is the plants themselves. So now we can speak confidently of the works of

Nature in their own right; and so the process of evolution begins. Even the waters 'gather themselves together into seas'. But they do so 'into one place'. This noun literally means 'room to stand up', and signifies theologically that the waters took form under the command of God (for God's Word is always Command), who then regards the seas as objects in their own right *vis-à-vis* the Word that created them; Jer. 5: 22; Job 38: 8, 10. And since the tense of the verb describes a process, our author is expressing the reality of the passage of time as well as that of space, in that both time and space are God's creation. Then, as with his former actions, it is only when God has first *separated* element from element that he next names them and thus identifies them. What we are learning therefore is of first-rate importance. It is that Nature herself has come into existence only through the incidence of crisis. The result is that only out of crisis, separation, have the millions of plant species on earth evolved throughout the ages.

Many of the species of plants were regarded by the Canaanites as members of their pantheon of gods. Israel lived alongside and along with those people over the centuries. But here these plants are mentioned to describe, not their being, but only their function within the plan of the Almighty.

Earth, however, takes a special place in the divine scheme. She is indeed 'Mother Earth'. 'Let the earth bring forth . . .'; and this reality remains in the thought of the great prophets in later years, e.g. Isa. 61: 11; Haggai 1: 11. God has made Nature both autonomous and free. In her freedom under God, therefore, she it is who is responsible for earthquakes and tidal waves. So it is not correct to call a natural disaster an act of God. For she is truly the Good Earth, in that she is also the mother of man, 2: 7.

So far as we know, God has particularized his plan upon this Mother Earth of ours alone. Scientists have not as yet established that on any other planet, the Moon, Mars, Jupiter, Venus, or on the farthest constellations, there is such a thing as spontaneous life. Earth alone, therefore, can be Mother to a human race. It is here, on earth, that God has particularized his great miracle, the creation of life. And to that end there appears already in the plan a differentiation within the vegetation. There is on the one hand the mass of green vegetation with which the earth is covered, and on the other hand there are also those herbs and fruit-trees that some day will provide food for man.

14–19 Any attempt to co-ordinate what follows with 'science' is quite unnecessary. This is because it is inconceivable that there could have been vegetation on earth before there was light and heat from the sun. Ancient man naturally knew that nothing can grow without light and heat. The heavenly bodies are mentioned only now for a definite reason. All the nations of the Near East, all of Israel's neighbours, worshipped the sun, moon, and stars as divine, Deut. 4: 19. The Pharaoh in Egypt was in fact the Sun incarnate. Here the heavenly bodies are so far from being divine that they are put to work by God to serve his plan. First of all he 'says' to them, and then he 'puts' them in their places. They exist only in order to serve the crisis significance of creation; they too are set to work separating the day from the night, and dividing up the passage of time into theologically significant signs and seasons, Jer. 10: 2; Isa. 7: 11; 2 Kings 20: 8–11; Ps. 104: 19. In themselves the sun, moon, and stars are of no significance, apart from being signs of the mighty plan.

We note, first, that the word 'lights', v. 14, is not the word we met at v. 3. It is the word used of the lamps that found their place in the Tabernacle, and which were placed there to aid man in the worship of God, Ex. 35: 14. At Ex. 25: 37 Moses was to make seven 'lights' as aids to worship, seven being the number of planets that shine in the sky and which are visible to the naked eye. We note, secondly, that the planets are called 'signs'. Naturally, these bodies can act as signs only to sentient beings; and so the narrative implies that God uses the heavenly bodies to interpret his own nature and plan to man, and thereby denies that the planets have any special significance in themselves. For example, as these bodies swing around the heavens – and around the earth – at clearly defined intervals, they become signs that God has sanctified time and the passage of time and has brought time within the total plan which is now unfolding. Thus they swing around the heavens not at their own will but in accordance with the laws which *God* has established for their regulation. Thirdly, the word for 'seasons' has nothing to do with the climate or weather. It is the word used for the religious

festivals which God had by now given to Israel, and through
which Israel was to serve God. In a word, this vast universe
with its galaxies of exploding stars and Milky Ways is so far
from being divine in itself, or even the source of mere astro-
logical speculation, that it exists, not for itself, but for little man,
who has his home on this one small planet within the vastness.
Yet not first of all for man in himself; rather for the glory of God
which only man can render. The reality that God has put the
heavenly bodies *in their place* (in the colloquial meaning of the
expression) is shown by the use of the verb in the singular '*let
there be* lights'. By this means we are shown that God has
created them all in one mere act as Lord of all.

20–23   The ocean too is free to produce unlimited swarms
of fish and the air is free to produce prolific swarms of birds. It is
interesting that the verb used here has also the secondary sense
of quick movement, surely apt for describing a shoal of fish or a
flight of birds. These swarms represent the unbounded interest
and care and concern of the living God.

Then next God creates, *bara* (as at 1:1) mammals. Some of
the larger animals were originally gods, envisaged in the shape
of whales, crocodiles, and so on. But ocean and air are under
orders. Chaos cannot produce life. One basic regulation that
God lays down for his world of wild creatures is the rule of sex;
otherwise they could not reproduce themselves. Birds in the air
and salmon and eels in the sea, therefore, follow the mysterious
rule of the migratory instinct and mate only at the end of a
mighty journey. But creation enjoys being under orders, glad
that it is not left to chaos, as we learn from the dancing of the
dolphin and the song of the birds. Is this a natural result of their
freedom under rule? This must surely be so, in that God has
blessed their reproductive processes. In fact the blessing appears
in the form of a promise. It is God's will that these creatures
should swarm and enjoy their life together. So the word 'fill'
means just that – fulfil the command of God.

And since man too is an animal, we note also that God's
blessing upon man is that he too should swarm, even as did
Israel under the evil rule of the Pharaoh in Egypt, Ex. 1:7.
That is why pagan Egypt could not appreciate the prolific care
and concern of God for Israel, and consequently regarded
Israel's growth under God's blessing as comparable with a

plague of lice or locusts. As the number of animals grows, so is the grace of God all the more visible till it becomes clear that he is concerned even with the fall of but one sparrow, Matt. 10: 29.

24–25 The world of mammals too *had* to come into existence, because God *said* so; 'and it was so'. However, the animals this time are a product of Mother Earth and do not receive a blessing direct from God. They receive their powers of procreation only from Nature, even though 'the earth is the Lord's, and the fulness thereof', Ps. 24: 1, and though God owns it as his possession, Ps. 50: 10–12; Haggai 2: 8. The types of animals named included those, as we have said, that were even monsters of evil, named in the OT as Rahab, Isa. 30: 7, Leviathan, Job 3: 8; Ps. 74: 14; Isa. 27: 1, or the Dragon or Serpent, Job 7: 12; Ps. 74: 13; 148: 7; Isa. 27: 1. We are to note that these monsters are all theological picture representations of the original monster of chaos. So their mention leads us to recognize that even 'the powers of evil' maintain their freedom to sport in the ordered realm of God's and nature's ocean. Even they are *good for* God's plan. Not only so, even when evil becomes incarnate, it still maintains its freedom. Isaiah invites his temple audience to regard the Egypt of their day as the incarnation of this Rahab, Isa. 30: 7; Ex. 7: 9. And Deutero-Isaiah sees the drowning of Pharaoh and his army when Israel came out of Egypt as, once again, God's act in cutting Rahab in pieces. Thus God's action in cleaving the Red Sea in order to save (that is, to re-create) his people was a historical representation of his primal act in the beginning when he split *tehom* in order to create the universe, Isa. 51: 9–10.

We are now able to say with confidence that the God whom we meet here is not merely the Almighty who rules or even overrules; he is the God who creates and orders his great plan by making use of the darkness and chaos so as to bring good *out of* evil, life *out of* death. Thus the creation story is basic to the whole biblical revelation. It shows us a God who does not create only in the beginning, but a God who never ceases to create and to re-create. So he is the Author not just of the idea of everlastingness, he is the Author of redemption, for this is only another name for re-creation. The seal of such revelation lies in the fact that creation does not end with the creation of man, but in the revelation that the end of the whole creative process is

actually known to God as Rest, 2:2. The biblical literalist
misses the whole point of this chapter therefore if he thinks of it
as only the story of creation. For rather it is a theological-
picture-description of the meaning of God's redemptive plan for
his whole creation, and the creation is really the eschatological
sign of the world to come.

26-31   'Then God said "Man", and there was man.' Man
is not an individual. He is not even male plus female. If man,
then, is to be in the image of God, then God himself must be
understood in plural terms. So 'Let us . . .' says God to his
corporate 'self'. The act thus takes place only after consultation
and deliberation. It is as if God were asking 'Will this really be
for the best?' For the creation of man is a more momentous act
than that recorded at 1:1. Even though man is born of Mother
Earth, 2:7(J), he is not to be equated *with* creation. For he
represents a special act of creation. Whereupon God addresses
the man and the woman equally as 'you'; he does not so
address the animals.

Much discussion has taken place on the meaning of the words
'image' and 'likeness'. In the first place the two words seem to
represent a double emphasis, just as *tohu* and *bohu* do in 1:2
('without form and void'). In English we can make the same
kind of emphasis in such a phrase as 'kith and kin'. Secondly, it
would appear from the context that 'image' means 'copy', that
is to say, the word is the writer's pictorial term for our abstrac-
tion 'moral correspondence'. He is declaring thereby that God
has made man morally free by giving him a will of his own. He
can thus use his own reason so as to be able to know and love
God freely. It does not appear that 'image' means that man is
made to look like God. Rather man is made *to do what God does*.

'What is man for?', then, is the question that arises here. The
answer is to be found only when we learn what God is for. This
surely is an astonishing thing to say. Yet God had already given
Moses the answer to that question, that God is for – us, Ex. 3:
12. In light of this divine statement we are not to seek from this
verse a biblical anthropology, for the emphasis is not on the
scientific nature and origin of man. Rather it is upon God, and
upon his act of grace. We are even left with the second question,
'What did it mean for God to create man?'. 'What a sign of
God's love', said Rabbi Akiba (Aboth III, 8) 'that man was

created in his image. What still greater love, that he was told of being created in his image!'

Later on we find that God addresses man, and talks to him as a friend, or as a husband talks to his wife. In Ps. 8: 4 God 'visits' man, a thing he does not do to the animals or to Nature. So the word 'image' stands for the unique connexion that the mysterious and incomprehensible Creator has established with man, not man with God. On the one hand, man is ranged along with all the other creatures that God has made; on the other hand he stands *beside* God as God's friend, and *confronts* the rest of creation from that stance. In other words, man's humanity rests upon his likeness to God.

Again, God did not make a man and a woman. He created, *bara* (as at 1: 1), Man. In this section of the chapter this verb is actually employed three times, clearly to emphasize the opposite of the way in which Israel's Canaanite neighbours used their imagination. For they fashioned their gods in the image of man, even as did the Greeks and the Romans, even as does modern man now. He betrays himself when he says for example, 'If I were God, I would do this and this . . .'. Genesis denies the validity of man's imagination. For one thing, when man imagines his gods, he makes them male and female. The present-day feminist movement repeats this Canaanite falsehood.

Yet Man alone is not Man; we shall soon see how he searched for completeness from amongst the animals. Each of the two sexes merely represents Man, one malely, one femalely. So this final act of creation is a revelation of the love of *God*, in that he has made Man capable of mutual love, and as one *with whom he can share his love*. Man is the one to whom God can say: 'Son of man, stand upon your feet, and I will speak to you', Ezek. 2: 1. Everything then about man in this passage points to God.

The statement that man is to have dominion over the birds, beasts, fish, the soil and even the snakes, has a very positive content. For the verb 'subdue' means to 'create order'. The phrase 'to rule the animals', says Westermann, is that used of the sun and moon; these were given power, we saw, to rule the day and the night, that is to say, the day and the night *depend* upon their rule. So too the fate and future of the animal creation is to depend upon man. The animals are not there merely for man's use, and man may not exploit them. This responsibility does not extend to the earth's vegetation, for vegetation is not 'living' as are the animals, v. 21. So man is meant to continue to re-create, even as God does, in that he is the image of God. Yet, even as he multiplies his sheep and his cattle, man is to remember that he does so only as a steward of the earth, for God alone is Lord. As the last creature to be fashioned, man is not *above* creation; rather, he is bound to it. Ps. 8 speaks of the fact of man's dominion over God's creatures with awe. In the Psalm all praise is given, not to man, but to God himself.

God then blesses Man, male and female together, and then he *says* the Word: 'Be fruitful and multiply'. Clearly God has blessed the sexual union that alone procreates the next genera-tion. Childbearing is the will of God. Sexuality is God's gift to man. Man's sexual organs are therefore to be used only at God's command; he has given them to man not for purposes of lust or self-gratification, but for the furtherance of his plan.

This whole paragraph ends on a new note. This time God sees everything he has made, 'and behold it is *very* good'. Chaos has now become order. But that is not by any means the end of God's plan. All that he has now created is sitting in position, so to speak, and is good *for* – what? We are not yet told. For all history must run its course before we can know the answer to that question. But evidently it is all there *for* the plan of God which is yet to unfold, a plan which will now include the self-will in freedom of that Man who is made in the image of that God who has freely chosen to create Man. But since the plan is good, it must be good for *whatever* the future may hold. Perhaps this idea is expressed by a very subtly used word. Before this we have had 'There was evening and there was morning, a third day . . . a fifth day'. But here we have *the* sixth day, for it was the most important day of all. Each day is a section of space and time, and God therefore regards each day as 'today'. Thus each 'today' is ultimately significant, for God, and thus must be also for man, Ps. 95: 7.

2: 1–3   In the meantime there is *shalom*, harmony, perfec-tion, for the number seven is the perfect number. The OT, notes Bonhoeffer, sees this perfection in man's case as having a share of earthly posessions, a vine and a fig tree, many children, long life, friendship, love, wisdom, beauty, honour, and political freedom. This earthly conception of perfection is a continual thorn in the flesh to the pietist. The pietist, he continues, even thinks that because of this view the OT is inferior to the NT. But Jesus, he says, affirmed life. He said that he had come to offer it 'and more abundantly'. For all these good things give man joy, peace, and security. God rejoices, we may add, in the nature he has made, Ps. 104: 31; Job 38: 7. This vital life is to be found everywhere. 'All the host of them' is how man understands this vital life either in terms of the natural elements Ps. 103: 21, or in terms of angels, 1 Kings 22: 19, or as the very cosmos itself, Isa. 34: 1. And so this vast area of life, including what Paul calls 'the principalities and powers in the heavenly places', God has invited to rest in him. God's rest is thus the eschatological significance of his work of creation.

Did God work on the seventh day, is a question that the Rabbis once discussed agitatedly: 'And on the seventh day God finished his work'. It would appear that God made creation complete by his act of resting. For God knows satisfaction in his work, and invites the heavenly host to find it too. By blessing the moment of the completion of his work God revealed that his Rest gave meaning to all the steps taken in creation, including the use even of darkness, and so of the fact that human life now depends upon death. The word for work is that used in the Fourth Commandment. It is related to the word for messenger. Thus it indicated (B. Jacob) the realization of a thought, desire, and intention. And so we learn that if God finds satisfaction in work, then man's work too is important, in fact work *matters*. And so *God's* rest from work is our rest, a rest which we may enter into at his invitation, Ps. 95: 11. It is not a rest of our own devising, which may be mere laziness and lack of purpose. It is this total satisfaction which God alone can know and then bestow. That is why God not only blessed the seventh day, he also hallowed it, that is to say, he regarded it as *qadosh*, holy, or as we have said, as the eschatological significance of the other six days. Some scholars want to translate here by a pluperfect of the verb, viz. 'On the seventh day God had completed his work'. But this suggestion is irrelevant, in that we are not dealing with a historical event.

The noun Sabbath does not occur here. This passage is not 'the origin of the Sabbath'. The Sabbath is a festival rooted in history. Later we shall discuss the relationship between this whole Prologue which offers us Theology in pictures, and the historical realities which give birth to it.

How different all this is from what the word *rest* means in the Babylonian creation epic *Enuma elish*. There the various gods try to *achieve* rest, always being frustrated by the noisy activities of the lesser gods, or by the fact that there is no place for them to rest. Finally the only way they can reach the rest is by killing off mankind in a flood. On the contrary, as we shall see later, the biblical God finds rest *in* Noah, even as the latter floats on the flood that God himself has caused. As von Rad says, this rest of the biblical God is returned to the world. The world is complete now, indeed, but that only means that it is completely ready for God to use in the next step of his plan. And God is at rest about that, no matter what may eventuate as a result of man's free will. So, most wondrous, man is meant to share in God's own rest.

Genesis One, then, is a complete item in itself. It is written in order to *create faith* in the reader, its power to do so being in the reality that it itself is revelation. It is a revelation of the meaning of *all things*, of darkness as well as of light. In a staggering plainness and brevity, as Westermann claims, it sets forth God's original plan for life, for meaning, for direction, for shape, God himself revealing his supervision over all. It is not meant to be an answer to our question, 'How did God create?' Rather, it answers the question, 'Why did God create?' God means it to be a general revelation for our sakes, such as will then enclose the special revelation about which the rest of the Bible speaks.

Thus there is no suggestion that the Creator is known to man only through faith. The story leaves open the possibility of unfaith. The biblical revelation puts little emphasis on the need to command men to believe. Rather what it does is to summon men to *remember* what God has done. And what God has done only begins with creation. God continues his revelation in his redemptive acts, that of the Exodus, Ex. 13: 3; and of the Cross, 1 Cor. 11: 25. This is because all is of grace. Man does not need to co-operate in his own salvation. God alone is the Author, the Creator of that.

4a   P's statement ends with the words: 'These, then, are the generations of the earth and the heavens ...'. We might

translate by: 'These are the line of . . .' or 'the history of . . .'.
The colophon occurs several times in P's material. Since 5: 1
reads, 'These are the generations of mankind . . .', we are to see
that chapter 1 has dealt, quite literally, with the first chapter in
God's creative plan. Humanity, we see, is *descended* from the
heavens and the earth (B. Jacob); so this metaphor joins nature
with history. First must come the history of the *place* where God's
plan is to work out. Only secondly can there take place the
history of that humanity for whom God has set a place on the
earth.

This amazing piece of theological writing, then, had to be 'got
over' to the ordinary man in Israel, and so not remain the property of the educated priestly class. How to do this for an
illiterate people was a real question. Some scholars believe that
Israel naturally copied the ways of some of her neighbours. The
Babylonians, for example, recited their creation myths to
accompany the re-enactment by actors of the *akitu*, New Year,
festival. Israel, on the other hand, celebrated her New Year
about the end of September for the space of the seven days of
the Feast of Tabernacles. Perhaps the great crowd of worshippers at the Jerusalem Temple were enabled on each of the seven
days to hear this *theological* narrative spoken out loud. For it
represents the basis on which their whole faith in the God of
creation and of salvation was laid and sustained. And so it became a liturgy of rejoicing in the love of God.

CHAPTER 2

THE UNIQUENESS OF MAN

4b–7   This chapter, along with chapters 3 and 4, originates from a period half a millennium before chapter 1. It is therefore as different from chapter 1 as Mark's Gospel is from John's. Chapter 2 also gives an account of creation. The framework of P's thinking that we have in chapter 1 seems to belong in Mesopotamia, since it reveals the rich background of the creation myths of the peoples of that area; and, as we saw, it possibly saw the light actually when Israel was held captive in Babylonia. J's background, on the other hand, reveals an environmental background of desert and oasis, such as is found only a matter of miles from the city of Jerusalem.

Like 1 : 1–3 this account of creation also begins by employing a series of subordinate clauses before reaching the first verb. P had begun with 'In the beginning of God's creating . . .'. J says merely, 'When . . .', for that is all that 'In the day that . . .' means. P's first verb occurs only at v. 3, 'God *said* . . .'. J's is 'Yahweh Elohim *fashioned* . . .'. P regards the creation of man as the crown of God's activity. J tells here of the formation of man as God's first act. Each source is thus making a theological statement of its own, each in its own way declaring that man is the prime object of God's creative activity. That is why J can say quite blithely that God created man before he created any food for man to eat.

Throughout much of the OT period the concept of chaos was pictorialized in two ways. The first one we have already seen at 1 : 2, that of a hurricane in the primal ocean whirling in total darkness. The other one, which we only mentioned in chapter 1 in passing, is a more understandable picture to a people that did little ocean voyaging; it found its background in desert, or at least in wilderness country. Moreover, we are to remember that the Wilderness of Judea began only a few miles from the city of Jerusalem; any citizen could go and take a look at it, and wonder at the mystery that there could be such a place as a water-less, virtually vegetationless void. At v. 6 we meet with the word 'mist'. Before the significance of the image described here was recognized, the Greek and Latin translations both used 'spring'. But it is much more likely that we are to understand the word to mean a damp patch of soil where water is oozing up from below. In the early morning this phenomenon would produce a mist. Anyway, the meaning 'mist' is what we find in the cognate term in the Akkadian language. This water would not come from a river – for no rain had fallen as yet. It was rather a seepage from the primal ocean under the earth. This dampness there-after spread over 'the whole face of the ground'. What we have pictorialized here then is the miracle of life appearing in a desert, beginning with an oasis and then spreading and showing even flowing water as in the case of Ezekiel's mystical river that flowed from the Temple in Jerusalem through the Wilder-ness of Judea and that ended by giving life even to the Dead Sea, Ezek. 47: 1–12. The Phoenician cosmogony of Sanchuniaton, a knowledge of which has come to us through the Greek-speaking scholars Berossus and Eusebius, represents this kind of thinking. The Hebrews, living next door to the Phoenicians, would know well their myths and philosophies.

God now 'fashions' man. He needed damp earth, of course, to produce a human shape. The verb is that used of a potter as he handles the damp clay on his rotating wheel; cf. Jer. 18: 5. And so God made man out of the earth. Once again, therefore, it is Mother Earth which produces man's body, Ps. 139: 15; 1 Cor. 15: 47. Man is flesh, with all the possibilities of desire, of knowledge, of failure, of error, to which human flesh is heir.

The word Yahweh ('Lord' in AV and RSV) is the name re-vealed by God himself to Moses at Ex. 6: 2 f. It is the name used throughout all J's material. Since Israel knew Yahweh as the God who had redeemed them from slavery in Egypt, he was in very deed their own Saviour God. P had spoken of Elohim, 1: 1, using the Semitic root that describes the divine Being in general. Here, however, we find both names placed together, an unusual combination, almost peculiar to Gen. 2–3. (The combination is found again at Ex. 9: 30.) It may well be that the final editor of the book of Genesis devised this means of linking the two creation stories together, to make it clear that they both describe the activity of the one and only God.

'Adam was not yet there to work the *adamah*', v. 5. The two words, to the Hebrew mind, were clearly related, the word ground being the feminine form of the word for man or humanity. The root meaning of *adam* may be 'red', the colour of the soil of much of the Arabian peninsula. It is only modern western man who thinks of calling himself white. The Chinese call European man pink. This popular etymology is important, moreover. For the emphasis is made that man is no god. He is not like the semi-divine beings of the Greeks and the Indians. Man is of the earth, earthy, a lump of clay, *in the first place*. God actually fashions him into what he is *with his own hands*; no demiurge, this tells us, has come between God and his creation. The picture represents the thought, the care, the concern, the eternal purpose of God for *me*. But it also describes two other important ideas. First, that God has authority over me, and second, that all men are necessarily brothers. Michelangelo's fresco on the ceiling of the Sistine Chapel, showing the finger of God not quite touching the finger of man, represents some of the depths of revelation seen in this passage. Though man is created by the finger of God, yet man is not God, but a free, independent being in his own right. On the one hand, Nature obeys God, because that is the law of its existence. It cannot act otherwise. It knows no will, only necessity (B. Jacob). On the other hand, God has created man free.

But that is not all. God takes this clay effigy and breathes into its nostrils the breath of life. Like the word Elohim, 'God', 'life' too is a plural noun. Life cannot be defined only from its manifestation in one dog, one mouse, one man. The characteristic adjective used throughout the OT along with the noun 'God' is 'living'. The God of Israel is the living God, in contradistinction to the gods of men's dreaming. Even as the unlimited greatness of God is shown by a plural noun, so too the unlimited nature of life is expressed in plural form. For life is of God, of the living God. 'And man became a living *nephesh*.' No longer is he merely clay. The very life of the living God is in him. Nor is he now a mere body. The Hebrew language possesses several words for the human body. But this word *nephesh* does not mean body. Equally it does not mean soul. Man is not a soul residing

in a body. Nowhere in the Bible is it ever suggested that man
'has an immortal soul'. In this regard the biblical faith is in
total opposition to the religions of man. Even the Targ.Onk. is
wrong here to translate by 'a talking spirit'. Rather, as we must
compromise by declaring, man is an animated body. This word
nephesh seeks to express what we mean by a total person, man as
body, soul, and spirit, a psycho-physical self, Ps. 104: 29–30;
Job 34: 14–15. But more, it expresses also the idea of man in
community, a man in relation to others in all the various possible capacities of parent, friend, employer, servant, etc. [See my
A Christian Theology of the Old Testament, sec. ed., 1964, pp. 33,
89, etc.; and Joh. Pedersen, *Israel, I and II*, pp. 99–181.] We
note that even when a man has died he is still regarded as a
nephesh, Num. 6: 6; 19: 13, and not as either a dead *body*, or as a
disembodied *soul*. The verbal forms of this noun *nephesh* all
express the idea of 'refreshing oneself', of renewing one's vitality,
and such like. Even an animal, we should note, is a *nephesh*,
2: 19, though it is never said that God has breathed into its
nostrils the breath of life.

8–9   In chapters 2, 3 and 4 most of the names that occur
bear a meaning. Yet some of these names have altered over the
ages, and we are not sure now what all of them represent. Eden
is a word meaning delight. This gives us a clue to realizing that
we are in an allegorical world similar to that found in Bunyan's
Pilgrim's Progress. This garden which God planted is not there
merely for God to enjoy. God's act in creating it is an act of
grace. He has produced the garden for man to enjoy and its
fruits are meant for man's nourishment and health. As in the
previous chapter, we are justified once again in making use of
the word 'for'. What is Eden *for*? we wonder. To call the Garden
Paradise, as the LXX does, is not correct. A paradise was a
hunting estate meant *for* an eastern monarch.

The name Eden occurs elsewhere, e.g. 2 Kings 19: 12;
Isa. 37: 12; Ezek. 27: 23; Amos 1: 5. The Genesis Eden, however, is not to be identified with any of these references. J would
know of the existence of these place names. But by putting Eden
in the *east* he is doing what P does in chapter 1. He is fixing the
Garden of God on this planet earth, so that we are not to describe it either in heavenly or in paradisal terms. Since Hebrew
and Aramaic use only one word for our two words, 'space' and

'time', it is understandable that the Targ.Onk. comes to trans-late the 'idea' of Eden by the phrase 'long ago' in the far-off unknown. Eden rather is a picture of God's good and kindly plan for man. It describes the experience possible to man of fellowship with God within space and time, yet out of which it is possible for man to be driven. The very trees that grow in the Garden reflect man's delight in the beauties of nature and in the taste of good food; cf. Ezek. 47: 12. J does not need to say with P that 'God saw that it was good'. He just describes the Garden as actually being good.

Throughout what follows there appears to be a conflation of two narratives; in one of them the tree of life is at the centre of the garden, in the other the tree of the knowledge of good and evil. Here the editor mentions both trees, and makes use of both as the story proceeds. It is not basically important for us to analyse the text of the two narratives. What we want to discover is what the editor makes of the two as he employs the symbolism of them both in the final form of his narrative that we possess.

He names the tree of life first. The symbolism of that is that God's gift to man of life is his basic, central gift. Without life man could not experience delight, and could not have fellow-ship with God. Moreover, if life is in the midst of the Garden, then it is God who is central to the story being told, not man. This reality is taken up in the NT at John 1: 4; 3: 15–16; Rev. 2: 7; 22: 2, 14.

The meaning of the tree of knowledge of good and evil has been widely debated by scholars. Some suggest it means that God has given us what we call a conscience. But that would be to ignore the little word 'for'. At Deut. 1: 39 we see that the phrase refers to children who are too young to know either what is good *for* them, or what is bad *for* them. We warn our children: 'Do not put your finger in the fire; it is not good *for* you'. Almost certainly the phrase 'good and evil' suggests the total range of knowledge that is possible to man, knowledge from A to Z, as we might say, or, on the analogy of an electric battery, from the positive to the negative pole. How this comes to mean 'the place of responsible obedience' we shall see later. Meanwhile man is given the task of tending the Garden. God himself works; consequently he did not create man to be idle, as we shall see at v. 15; yet only after we have examined the inset at vv. 10–14.

10–14   Already at 2: 6 we have been made aware that there can be no life without water. This present inset therefore pictures God's gift of the water of life in terms of a river, flowing out of Eden, to make the rest of the world also into a garden. Thus, not just from this the second chapter of the Bible onwards, but even in chapter 1: 3, the concept of God's own life being known in terms of mission is revealed. This one river then divides into four, and these now flow to the four points of the compass. Next, the particularism of the biblical revelation is made apparent. Although we are speaking in symbols, these rivers are meant to be geographically definable within the known world of ancient near-eastern man. The Tigris and the Euphrates we know. What Pishon and Gihon represent bring us only to guesswork. The name Pishon may have come from a verbal root that describes the vital activity of young creatures, and so is a good parallel with Gihon, which means a bubbling, gushing spring of water. So what we now have are two historical rivers, and two symbolic rivers, as if to show us that we are to think in terms of the two areas of theological enquiry at once. For Pishon and Gihon have 'bubbled up' from an underground source, v. 6. Thus they speak of the life-giving grace of God emerging from the waters of chaos.

The name Havilah occurs at 10: 7, 29; 25: 18. It may be an area in Arabia; and it may also mean sandy or desert-like. Instead of 'flows around', *Tor* suggests 'winds through', though both the Egyptians and the Babylonians supposed that there was a river that went right round the earth. Bdellium may be a kind of stone (cf. LXX, *anthrax*); others believe it is a kind of transparent gum, wax-like; in Assyrian it means a kind of resin. Cush probably refers to the geographical area we know as the Sudan – but the vast area south of Egypt was an unknown world to the ancient Israelites.

15–17   Eden is evidently not a pleasure garden for mere sensual enjoyment. People have pictured it as a place of peacocks and picnics. Rather, man is obliged to till the Garden and guard it, presumably from foxes and other marauding animals. In a semi-tropical land a garden goes 'back to nature' in no time. Man's task is to keep it ordered. Man's destiny therefore is shown to be a sober pleasure in creative work and in obedience to God.

In this situation the Lord God 'lays a command' upon man. So we discover that human freedom is meant to be a proper relationship between obligation and unrestricted enjoyment. And we go on to note that knowledge without obedience is perverse, and such perversion can only lead to death.

The command has a boundary. In raising children parents set boundaries to their children's freedom. 'You may freely play anywhere in the garden, children; but you must not go out onto the street. For if you do, you will die.' The child is glad of the boundary. It gives him a sense of security. He knows for sure that inside the garden he is safe. Yet the restriction itself leads to curiosity. Why might it be dangerous to go through the garden gate? Thus we see in this theological picture that God gave man freedom to obey or not to obey, freedom to say 'Yes' to life, or to say 'No' to it. Joel eschatologizes this element in the command of God by speaking of the Day of the Lord in terms of the 'Valley of Decision', Joel 3: 14. No explanation of this restrictive command is given apart from a hint at the prodigality of God's love. Yet man knows only too well what its restrictive nature entails.

18–25   This section now expounds the content of the command. 'It is not good (*for* God's plan) that the man should be alone', declares the Lord God himself. Much damage has been done in the past to the man–woman relationship because of the mistranslation of these words as they appear in the AV, where the word 'helpmeet' occurs. There it reads as if the woman were only an adjutant to the commanding officer. The Hebrew, however, means 'a complete *vis-à-vis*', a helper who fits him exactly, his 'opposite number'. And so it describes an intellectual equal, a fellow-labourer, one who will share with him in the work of the Garden, and complement him in the task they are meant to do as a team of two. So humanity, now described as 'man-plus-woman', is quite properly expressed as a plural noun, because together they are in the image of *elohim*, the 'plural' God.

In order to clarify what this 'opposite number' means, the writer has first to show what woman is *not*. She is not an animal. Man has received God's permission to organize and handle the animal world. This is J's way of declaring what P has expressed at 1: 28. Man is able to describe the difference between a camel and an elephant. This ability to describe is an aspect of the naming of each separate species; and so man gives each variety of living creatures its separate identity. There are tens of thousands of species of moths; but we do not begin to notice the differences between them till we seek to name them. Out of the mystery of the primal chaos man has the task of producing order. What we find here is what Linnaeus did when he first classified the earth's plants and living creatures two hundred years ago. But man passes by the animals as he searches for fulness of life. What he is looking for is an experience that can be gained only as the gracious gift of a gracious God.

The word for 'deep sleep' does not describe natural sleep. It speaks of the coma into which a dear one may fall, and which shocks us as we stand by him helplessly. For the condition of coma reminds us of the whole range of non-being, horror, and death which lies just under the surface of our human lives. Man's body has already been fashioned from the soil. Now it is to be woman's turn. She is to be fashioned as an extension of that body, from the point nearest to his heart. But once again this new creation does not happen as a smooth process of evolution. Once again we witness an act of fundamental crisis, one with the crisis we found to be basic to this mysterious universe, 1:6.

It is therefore over against this horrifying background that God 'introduces' the female to the male. The latter's response is thereupon one of delighted satisfaction: 'This, *at last . . .*' is really the completion of myself. He has already sought for possible companionship with every other creature in the Garden. She alone, however, gives him total satisfaction simply because she *is* of the same flesh as himself. 'She is neither in front of me, nor behind me', he declares; 'she is *beside* me.' God had already made man to be such that he could commune with God; now man has received God's gift of woman as one with whom he can also find communion. Yet, by his very nature, man is never satisfied. He is always restless, ever seeking answers to ultimate questions. Because this is so, God therefore helps him find the answers through the self-emptying and mutual love and commitment that has now become possible for both of them as they strive towards the future *together*. This act of God, then, is another act of grace divine.

The man now names the woman. That is to say, he knows

that he has authority over her, even as he knows the difference between one animal and another. But at this point the meaning of the word 'know' must be looked at. He now knows her even as he knows himself in an experience of equality which he, not she, initiates. To put this in terms of our present-day culture, Mr. John Smith invites a woman to becomes Mrs. John Smith. He does so, because he believes that together with her, as two Smiths, they will find in a shared experience the irrepressible joy which he knew alone when he first saw her as a separate entity. He will now compound his first happy dependence upon God through this new experience of mutual companionship.

The rib motif appears in the very ancient Sumerian myth, where it occurs as a pun. For the goddess who was created to heal Enki's rib was called Nin-ti, 'the lady of the rib', or 'the lady who makes alive'. So there too the woman is *built* out of man's essential stuff. How different, however, is the Genesis story. Employing unashamedly the cultural thought-forms of his day, J has been able to turn mere myth into theology-in-a-picture. The latter now proffers the ultimate answer to the perennial human question of the relation between the sexes. Thus the man says: 'She shall be called *ishsha*, because she was taken out of *ish*.' (These words are related to each other just as are *adam* and *adamah*, 2: 7.) We are fortunate that in English we can render this connectedness, this oppositeness, this complementarity of the two sexes, by the words *woman* and *man*. The French language cannot do this, however, with its words *femme* and *homme*. Later, the man calls the woman by still another name, a name of hope, as we shall see when we reach 3: 20. And so the man uses his faculty of language to give, not just identity, but as Richardson says, actually life to the woman. Man had not been able to see God at work when God built the woman from his rib, but God had referred to him the joy of creating her identity in a name. It is in this sense therefore that we can speak of the man as being head of the (united) body. The woman's personality develops through fellowship with her husband from the flexible, open nature of the teen-age girl into the distinct personality who has helped him rise from obscurity to become a leader in the community. Only now, therefore, is the creation of man complete. Man is complete only when, in the image of God, the Creator, he himself creates the true marriage relationship.

Most commentators agree that v. 24 is a little sermon that was introduced into the text later on. But it illustrates the reality that no matter what may be the origin of a verse in the Bible the end result is that it is as truly canonical as any other; cf. Mark 10: 6–9. Monogamy here is God's expressly revealed will for man. Anything else, such as the four wives allowed to a Muslim, is not to be dismissed, negatively, as a mere concession to human lust. Positively, monogamy means that type of partnership which God himself knows in the unchangeable unity of his being in the Spirit through his Word; and so it means that this living comporate image of himself which he has fashioned may know the joy and deep contentment of 'resting', 2: 3, in their mutual companionship all the days of their life. At marriage a new creative unit is formed when both the man and the woman leave their father and mother behind, and the two become one flesh, cemented together (LXX). And so a home is created, something that is possible only where there is lifelong mutual fidelity. He belongs to her because she belongs to him. This is the doing of God the Father, says von Rad, when, at the wedding, he leads the bride to her waiting bridegroom. God is now not just Creator, far less is he fate or the *élan vital*. Instead the picture theology here demonstrates that it is quite correct to say that the first couple had no parents. For God is the Father in the marriage. God did not join two *spirits* together; the two became one *flesh* in sexual intercourse. Marriage is thus not a man-made contract. God introduces the woman to the man. Nor is it merely a social contract. For we are to remember that the great prophets, from Hosea onwards, saw the covenant relationship between God and Israel as one which they confidently described in terms of marriage; Hos. 1–3; Jer. 2: 1–3, 32; Isa. 62: 5. This marriage, however, is both monogamous and indissoluble, Isa. 50: 1. It exhibits therefore the kind of binding love which is described in the words of the popular hymn: 'O love, that wilt not let me go'.

God's unique choice of Israel is thus linked with this primal story. The woman limits the man, because he is limited to her in order to be one with her alone and not with another woman. In loving her he loves the limitation placed on him, as Bonhoeffer points out; and she by her faithfulness, helps him to bear the limitation. Fidelity is a necessary element in the integrity of the human spirit. Finally, in contradistinction to what the modern women's liberation movement *imagines* to be the biblical revelation, it is the *man* who is to leave home to live with the woman, and not the reverse. For his leaving home demands the greater sacrifice.

All this belongs to a different world of thought from the Greek myth of Narcissus, the male who fell in love with his own reflexion in a pool of water. It is that myth which, developed by the philosophies of the Greek nation and introduced to the civilization of Europe, has produced the long history of female degradation. But in Genesis the woman is not just the man's wife, she is also his life.

Clearly sexuality has no meaning of its own detached from its purpose within such a union. The sexual instinct, the erotic force, exists *for* the sake of the marriage, the family, relatives, the clan, the nation, the human race – all the elements that are basic *for* a picture of history. That is why, before the Fall, no sex-consciousness is exhibited. Yet, the words 'naked' and 'ashamed' clearly point to still deeper realities. Since man is the friend of God, he has nothing to hide from God. In the same way he has nothing to hide from the woman; for they are one. Man could thus stand unembarrassed before the gaze of God. Consequently he could do likewise before the eyes of his wife. Both the man and the woman here know the simplicity of heart of a child. That is why there is no need for them to become as little children; cf. Mark 10: 15. The reason why Jesus expressed himself in this way becomes apparent only in the next chapter.

CHAPTER 3

MAN'S REBELLION AGAINST GOD

1–7 This chapter is continuous with chapter 2. The story reverts to what we learned at 2: 19, that 'out of the ground the Lord God formed every beast . . . and whatever man called every living creature, that was its name'. The serpent is one of those living creatures. The P narrative expressly includes snakes, 1: 25. The animals are all 'living creatures', *nephesh ḥayyah*, and God creates them out of the ground, 2: 19. But man too is a *nephesh ḥayyah*, and him too God has fashioned out of the ground, 2: 7. In what follows we are shown that man's earthy nature can become very subtle at challenging the grace of God.

Our theologian now selects the snake out of all the animals that there are, because its low posture, that of crawling on its belly, pictorializes the animal nature of man. 'The snake approaches imperceptibly, tortuously, twistingly, and is the image of crookedness. It is apparently harmless, and yet is equipped with a terrible hidden weapon, slow and yet of lightning speed . . . an image of crafty seduction' (B. Jacob). God has already graciously informed man of the garden gate, and of the danger of death lying outside of it on the street, 2: 16–17. But instead of regarding God's Word of warning as a word of grace, man takes it to be a word of law. Man is annoyed that such a law should be laid upon him. It molests what he believes to be his divinely given freedom of choice. And so the animal part of him subtly seeks to subvert the gracious plan of God for his creature man, and in turn, through man for all God's creatures great and small. And yet it is not correct to speak of 'the animal part' of man. For man is one in being. It is man, whole man, who seeks to do this thing.

The word 'subtle' (which can mean 'nakedness' in Hebrew as well) describes the almost innocent inventiveness that we see in the young boy who places rocks on the railway track 'just to see what happens' when a train comes along. The boy is not innately wicked. He knows, however, that the adult world has erected a law against such inquisitiveness. Consequently he resists the fact of its being there. In his immaturity he does not see why he should not try out this ploy. Nowhere is it suggested in the text that the serpent is evil in itself. For God has made man's (animal-)nature 'good', 1 : 25. Far less ought we to read into this passage what many in the early Church took for granted, that the serpent is a manifestation of Satan.

Temptation begins with a mere insinuation of doubt. The serpent asks the woman a harmless question: 'Did God say . . . ?' Is the question in itself, however, not an expression of doubt? Would man's loyalty to God, who has given him his freedom, not be better expressed, when questions assail his mind, by such a phrase as 'Did not God say . . . ?' The latter question would quash the doubt. But the serpent in man opens the gate to doubting God's rule by asking the question, 'Is it really the case that . . . ?'

In contemporary Canaan the serpent was the symbol of the god Eshmun, the god of healing. Moses knew of its power when he lifted up the serpent in the wilderness, Num. 21 : 8–9. This Levantine theology later reached Greece; there the god Asclepius also was considered to be the serpent healer. Here our author, by choosing the serpent as his medium of revelation instead of any others of the animal creation, emphasizes the knife-edge relationship between the knowledge of good and the knowledge of evil of which man learns to be deeply conscious. The healing knife may at the same time be the killing knife, just as the plant grown in the garden, whose qualities are manufactured today as a useful drug, may be used to heal the mind or destroy the personality. The power released in nuclear fission may be used by man either to energize his civilization or to destroy it. 'Did God really say . . . ?' Yes, the serpent may in fact be man's benefactor, 3 : 22, but at such a cost that only God can handle the issue.

What we are reading here, as Bonhoeffer points out, is the first recorded conversation *about* God, carried on behind his back, so to speak, that has come down through history. Talking about God is often regarded as an exercise in religious enquiry.

But religion can be the very devil, as history again reminds us; it can be the opiate of the people, as Karl Marx declared. 'Is God good?' 'Is God jealous of man?' This is not a conversation *with* God; that would be an act of faith. As both Wellhausen and Bonhoeffer point out in connexion with this verse, in his search for reality, from pole to pole, from 'good for' to 'bad for', man shows that he is no longer obedient to God; instead he becomes, as he believes, 'better' even than God himself.

The serpent's question is really that most dangerous of all suggestions. It is couched as a half-truth, the form of expression beloved of propagandists of many a cause. What God had actually said was: 'You may freely eat of every tree of the garden, except for one'. Thus the serpent does not quote God accurately in his declaration, 'You shall not eat of any tree of the garden'. What we hear is a deliberate twisting of the truth in such a manner that the simple minded cannot see the fallacy in the statement. It is akin to the well-known logical fallacy found in the log kept by the First Mate: 'The Captain was sober today'.

Have any other 24 verses in all literature had quite such an impact on human thought *everywhere* as has this chapter? Is this not because the chapter deals with a reality that secular literature is afraid to take seriously, viz., that the nature and destiny of man is wholly bound up with man's relationship to God? Quite rightly the secularist rejects the notion that this chapter deals with the birth of human sin. The word 'sin' does not occur here at all. This fact must be recognized as an important aspect of revelation. For it is a fact that no such thing as sin exists as an element in itself within creation. Sin is not a 'thing' that can be described by a noun. Sin is always an activity. Sin is something that man *does*. If there were no man, then there would be no such thing as sin. What we 'see' here in this pictorial theology on the other hand is man in his freedom asking the kind of questions that may possibly lead on to acts of disloyalty and defiance. But he is asking them because he wants to know the truth. He cannot honestly see how he will die if he has been made in the image of God. And if he is made in the image of God, why should he remain a *creature* of God? All these seem to be legitimate questions for man to raise.

The great prophets, however, fully understand this view of

sin that we meet with here. They would repudiate as absurd the kind of preaching sometimes heard today: 'God loves you but hates your sin'. Isaiah's basic word for sin is rebellion. So aware is Hosea of Israel's self-centred rejection of grace that he can write of God: 'I will be to them like a lion. . . . I will tear open their breast . . . as a wild beast would rend them', Hos. 13: 7–8. The very early poem in Deut. 32, basic to the theology of much of the later literature of the OT, can declare: 'I kill and I make alive; I wound and I heal', Deut. 32: 39. In those passages there is no suggestion that God will merely destroy sin. For it is only when he destroys sinners that *sinners* can be healed and restored. Without this passage as the basis of Old Testament thought on this matter, the New Testament could not have given us a theology of the Cross.

2–3   The woman now proffers a bold and decisive answer to the serpent. She rejects the half-truth inherent in his question and replies by quoting the words of God *accurately*. 'God's commandment is not in question', she now says; 'in fact he has made us a generous offer' (von Rad). And yet the serpent's half-truth has done its work. It is the woman who uses in her answer the word 'fruit', not the serpent. This is because she is now envisaging what the serpent has not even spoken of explicitly. She does not mention the fact that God has called the tree 'the tree of the knowledge of good and evil'. She doesn't want to talk theology; what she wants is practical results. So she shows her exasperation by adding that she and her husband are forbidden even to touch the fruit. All this means that revelation is a reality. Somehow or other humanity knows the mind of God, difficult though it may be to define what revelation is and how it has taken place. Humanity *knows* that God is Lord, and that man ought to live in obedience to God's revealed will and plan for mankind, Deut. 29: 29; 32: 47; Hos. 4: 1. What man has learned throughout the ages is that he should live in a centrifugal relationship to God, that is to say, with his life revolving round God, with God at the centre – not the centripetal life he does live, as he flies off in every direction to the edges of existence, even as he pursues his own will and desires. It is *God*, however, who has planted the garden, and set up the hedge and the garden gate that separates the ordered world of obedience from the chaotic world of disobedience outside, and man cannot change the requirements to suit himself. Without rules life would indeed be chaos, just as without rules you cannot play a game of football.

4–5 The subtlety of the serpent becomes ever more apparent. It is an easy step to proceed from the half-truth to the deliberate suggestion that God is a liar. 'You will not die', he says to the woman, even though God had said distinctly that she would die, 2: 17. This desire to prove God a liar that resides in us all is of course bound up with the meaning of the phrase, 'knowing good and evil'. It rests upon the assumption – very obviously held in today's world – that man has a right to suspect the reality of the love of God.

As we saw at 2: 17, good and evil are the two poles of knowledge possible to man, covering both what is good for man and what is bad for him. God wants to protect man from the chaos that lies behind the light, 1: 1–3, a chaos which manifests itself in confusion, lawlessness, greed, selfishness, and pride. That is to say, chaos does not basically lie in the realm of the ethical, as we might suppose, but rather in the experiencing of the disruption of the man-made-in-the-image-of-God relationship. 'Knowing' good and evil describes more than an intellectual understanding of them; it means participation in them existentially; it means, in Hebrew, to be *able* to do what you want to do. Charles Manton, the notorious murderer, sought, it seems, to experience what God alone ought to be able to experience, but does not. He sought to discover what it feels like, experientially, to slit a human throat, and so in this way become a god himself. By becoming one with the Absolute, says his interpreter, R. C. Zaehner (*Our Savage God*, 1975), Manton arrived at a 'total experience' in which there is neither right nor wrong. This 'holy indifference', says Zaehner, cultivated by certain strands of mysticism can lead to a 'diabolic insensitivity' to human life. In contrast to this kind of eastern mysticism the whole biblical revelation is of a God who is *moral* and who, because he is such, *cares* for his creation and for man whom he has made in his own image.

The Targ.Onk. shies off making a literal translation of the words, 'You will be like God'; instead it says, 'like princes'. Targ-Jon. translates with the words, 'as mighty kings who know'. The Sam.Pent. employs the word 'angels'. The LXX has 'gods', by which term it probably means members of the divine court on high. Psalm 8: 4–5 asks the question, 'What is man?' and then continues with the words, 'Thou hast made him little less than God' – and again the LXX rendering of the Psalm has 'angels'. Yet P, at 1: 27, declares that this man, who has the power of the keys of the garden, is made in the image of God!

6 It is true that the woman is the first to be tempted. But she is also the first to resist temptation. Moreover, she does not lead the man astray, as is popularly believed. Rather, the man *gladly* agrees to her suggestion. v. 6 presents us with a realistic portrayal of what goes on in the human mind when temptation threatens. For discussion has now come to an end. Instead we meet with action. The word of the serpent has eventually and inevitably become 'flesh'. She is attracted by the charm of the forbidden. First she *looks*. There is no harm in just looking. Then she sees that the fruit is *good for* food. In other words, she has turned her *mind* to an examination of the fruit. Praise God for that. He created the trees in question. Then her appreciation of the fruit develops to include an aesthetic delight in it. Sight and taste work mutually together. In thus enjoying its attractiveness she is giving God the glory. Next she realizes that the fruit will add to her philosophical understanding of life. However, we note that this tree is no different in appearance from the other trees, 2: 9! Yet desire is born within her by just looking at *it*. Feeding the desire thereupon becomes more important to her than holding fast in loyalty to God's self-revelation of his loving nature and to her duty to the God who gave her life. Knowledge of the truth as it is in God is, as we have put it, a knife-edged experience. Our human life is very complex; we are given no easy answers to life's many problems.

Then follows a divine curiosity. She is nearly *there* now, she is nearly a god! 'What might happen if we split the atom?' 'What will eventuate, in this *God-given* world, if we mate a woman with a baboon?', cf. Lev. 18: 23. It is not wrong to seek knowledge and beauty. But is that what 'she' really wants? Is it not power that she is seeking? Power that is not concerned with moral issues? So we watch as her hand goes slowly out. No, she pulls it back. Out it goes again. With a quick movement finally she takes the fruit and puts it in her mouth. The awful act is described without emotion. Last of all she shares the fruit with her husband. That is to be expected; she is one flesh with him. It would be impossible for him not to be affected by her action. No matter how we understand the word 'sin', whether as a noun or a verb, it is as truly a mutual activity as is the reality of love. So man is now left with a sense of guilt, in his awareness that now *all* his relationships are disordered. This reality is perfectly outlined in chapter 11.

7   Finally both of them together experience the new world in mutual awareness. The fruit was indeed wonderful. It certainly changed man's whole universe of being. They had expected that, having covered the whole spectrum of sensual, intellectual, and aesthetic experiences possible to man they would have immediately become divine. The opposite, however, had taken place. They were completely changed indeed. But not only are they now poor, shivering, naked apes in that God can see them through and through, they also now *know* that they are naked, and that they are now no longer good even *for* each other. Each has now destroyed the limit of their mutual relationships, so that the limit the other now sets is not one of grace, but of discord (Bonhoeffer). That is to say, total love has disappeared. So now there can be sexual assault even within marriage, and uncreative sexuality is destruction *par excellence*. Of this, however, even natural man is aware, and he is ashamed that in all cultures there exist permissiveness and promiscuity. It is not beastly, of course, for a beast to be a beast. But it is beastly for a man to become a beast; cf. Dan. 4: 24–25, 33.

How gracious God is. He had first clearly warned the couple not to touch this tree. If they should do so, he had said, they would die, 2: 17. It was only after that that the serpent declared that God was lying, and that they would not die, 3: 4. The serpent, curiously, is right. They do not die. We can almost hear the debate in the mind of the Almighty such as Hosea reports: 'My people are bent on turning away from me; so they are appointed to the yoke, and none shall remove it'. Is that God's final word? Evidently not. 'How can I give you up, O Ephraim . . . my heart recoils within me, my compassion grows warm and tender, I will not execute my fierce anger . . . for I am God and not man', Hos. 11: 7–9.

How totally different the Genesis narrative is at this point once again from the myths contemporary with Israel's story. We may read the Adapa myth in ANET, pp. 101–103, to learn how that individual gives up both knowledge and life for man, so that in the end man keeps wisdom but not life. J is reasoning in quite a different world of thought, a world of revelation from a God of love. The ancient myths, as well as modern man, suppose that death means merely the destruction of the body. But here J understands death as separation from fellowship with God. The serpent was indeed right, factually and scientifically speaking. The couple did not die. But God was even more right. For from now on mankind walks in death, the death of that perfect harmony and fellowship with God which is God's gracious plan for him. And, as we shall learn later at 3:24, this theological, this spiritual death must continue indefinitely.

However, man refuses to believe that he is missing the fulness of life; he does not even desire it. And so man, male and female, one flesh in their ignorance of life, sew themselves aprons to hide the fact of their nakedness, their lack of uninhibited fellowship with God which they no longer enjoy.

We have already noted that the word 'sin' does not occur in this chapter. This is wisely done. Modern man, wearing his apron of fig-leaves, does not believe in the existence of sin. But he does believe in the other terms we have used, such as loyalty, beauty, and love. So in our re-interpretation of the self-revelation of God in terms of our own contemporary culture, we should pay heed to J and also avoid speaking of sin. Nor is there any mention of an apple in our narrative. The idea that the fruit that the woman took was an apple arose in the early Christian centuries when it was noticed that the Latin word for bad, *malum*, can also mean an apple.

One of man's relationships that is now disordered is that of his relationship within himself. God had created him to be a living *nephesh*, a whole unified personality. Into that wholeness his sex instinct fitted perfectly in place. But now it is out of place. The man cannot now look at the body of his wife in humble admiration. Instead he experiences a sense of shame in her presence, even as he experiences shame in God's presence. Sex, 'God's good idea', as we saw it to be at 1:27, is now no longer part of the harmony of life lived in dependence upon God in the Garden. And so sexual desire becomes, in a life lived apart from God, mere lust of the flesh.

8–13   Yet God accepts man as he is. God continues to walk in the Garden as if man still expected to have fellowship with him. It is not God who hides from man. It is man who hides from God.

Throughout the centuries right to the present day, in the warm lands of the Near East, it has been the custom for people to promenade the village street at the cool of the day, after work is over, and before retiring for supper and bed. Each individual smiles and bows to his acquaintances, and wishes them a good evening. God shares in this pleasant activity. But now man no longer appears on the village street. He has hidden himself among the trees of the garden. The inner disturbance he experiences is too acute for him to behave normally. The good fruit, God knows, has now turned to ashes in his mouth. Man has produced an evil situation, not by doing evil, but by misusing God's good plan for him.

Generously God gives the couple a chance to explain what has happened. God's nature is to be generous, long-suffering, kind and loving. He does not pre-judge an issue. He continues to accept the fact that man is a responsible being, with a point of view of his own that may, in fact, be fully justifiable.

At this point in the narrative we again meet with the majestic double title of 'the Lord God'. Humanity can hear the sound of this great God as he walks down the world's main street, invisible though he is to the human eye. So God and man are clearly still on the same plane, on the same ground of understanding. Yet the very fact that God is present unseen means that he is present *in judgment* while witholding himself *in person* from action before its time. But one sound from God is enough for man to lose all his titanism and to cower behind a tree.

9   God begins the conversation by recognizing the reality of the 'new birth'. He has to call out to man, now no longer at his side, 'Man, where are you?' [This is more accurate than 'Adam', for both the man and the woman are included in the name.] God calls to man to come out of his mood of self-reproach, secrecy, self-torment, and vain remorse. 'Son of man, stand upon your feet, and I will speak with you', Ezek. 2: 1. But man says, 'Sorry, God, my excuse is that I was drunk, drugged, infatuated, whatever'. Yet these are not valid excuses. God gently reminds him, 'Did I not command you ... ?'

At this point then three new elements in life make their appearance. First, fear. It was man's own doing that fear arose. Secondly, conscience too is born. And here we see that conscience is not the voice of God to sinful man, but man's defence against the voice of God. And thirdly, the idea of blaming someone other than yourself. Man, then, is still free. He is free to blame, free to defend himself against God, free even to attack God. There is no suggestion here either of the Muslim concept of *kismet* ('it is fated'), or of the Hindu doctrine of *Karma*. Nor is there any suggestion of a total 'fall' of human nature, as Westermann underlines. The Augustinian doctrine of total depravity may be a valid one, but it cannot be based upon the realities revealed in this chapter.

These three elements in human experience all occur without any mention of the serpent. The latter has now disappeared. He is no longer needed for the revelation of the reality about man that is taking place before our eyes. For man now, quite explicitly, is his own serpent.

God now asks a series of questions. He does not condemn. Rather, he gives man the opportunity to explain himself. There is a mean element in the blame that the man now utters. He insinuates that it was the fault of the Father of the bride that she had suggested he should join her in her act of disobedience. Clearly, in separating himself from God he had already separated himself from the woman. God's kindly gift to the man of the woman who was meant to be the delight of his eyes, this male now implies was behind all that had happened. Basically, then, we are shown that when a man's integrity is disrupted by a moral failure he does not face up to what he has done, but instead puts the blame on God for making the world the way it is.

The next act in the drama reveals that sin is contagious. The woman, learning from the man, now 'passes the buck' and puts the blame this time on human nature. She is more naïve than the man. She answers correctly! She puts the whole situation in a nutshell. She sums up reality with a cliché, as stupid and as naïve as are such sayings as 'Charity begins at home', or as 'My country right or wrong'. We recognize that there is no answer we can give to clichés such as these, in that it is not the words of the cliché but the basic attitude of the speaker that is at fault.

That is why God is 'stuck', dare we say, with the woman's silly answer. He does not turn from her and try to question the serpent. In fact the story really ends here. Consequently we are left in the half-light of the mystery in which we live and move and have our being, the mystery that we have no clear answer given us as to the origin of evil, or the nature of the serpent. At least we see that we must not blame the serpent for being subtle, nor blame this good Mother Earth for being unstable and sending us so many earthquakes or other natural disasters. What we do receive here, however, is the knowledge that God goes forward *from this point* to work in and through the instability of Nature and the self-centred choices of man to reach the goal he has set himself to achieve. Thus the weakness of the Creator God in face of man's rebellion is the most extraordinary reality revealed so far in these chapters. To use our colloquialism once again, Almighty God is now 'stuck'. What kind of a God is this, then, that we read of here? We can only give a tentative answer at this point by saying that God must now limit himself to act through law. Man had heard the commandment of God as a Word of grace; but he had then construed it as a Word of law. As a result, (1) the man had become annoyed at what he supposed was a threat to his freedom, (2) the woman had become a seducer, and (3) the serpent, that is to say human nature as it is in its freedom and innocence, had become an instrument of evil. So it is Law that is now the vehicle of the utterance of divine judgment.

14–15 The following six verses are in poetry. At some point in the transmission of the text this versification has taken place. Verse is easier to remember and to retell than prose, an important issue in pre-literate days. We remember, for example, how much of what the great prophets had to say was expressed in verse. In this respect we should note two things. First, as we have said, the prophets' utterances were meant to be memorable, so as to be passed on to children's children. But secondly, the speaker himself, as he expressed his mind in verse, was clearly experiencing a heightened consciousness and awareness of the mind of God. Again, this prophetic type of utterance, or *Gattung*, expressed in the form of a blessing or a curse, was regarded as being not mere words; it was an utterance that was in fact *potent*. As Isa. 55: 10–11 puts it, the Word of God cannot return to God fruitless, 'without accomplishing my purpose or succeeding in the task I gave it', NEB.

The potent Word of God is directed first at human nature. It states a fact, that man's animal nature is under a curse; cf. Isa. 25: 6; 25: 7; Dan. 9: 11; Rev. 22 :3. The idea of 'curse' recognizes the reality that man's world is actually in disintegration. The Hebrew for this is the opposite of *shalom*, integration, wholeness, peace. Yet since it is *God's* curse that is spoken here, in it God is also affirming this fallen world and announcing that it is just in this situation where man finds himself that man must live and work; cf. Deut. 32: 24; Micah 7: 17. And since this 'word' here is the Word of God, beneath all the terrible meaning of the curse there must of necessity rest a promise and a hope. Because even a curse from God is of his grace. His grace still rests upon this creature who has lost the vision of God, who has taken his journey into a far country, whose god is his belly, that is to say, who lives a life of sensuality. The beauty and holiness of the true marriage relationship that is implied at 2: 22–25 is beyond the understanding of natural man, even of 'religious' natural man, whether in Hindu, Buddhist, or Muslim lands, or in the West amongst the adherents of the many strange cults which rise and disappear from year to year.

Man's constant war with the snake is a picture of the clearheadedness of evil. The door to evil is always open. The woman implants the first antipathies into her child's mind even as he drinks her milk. Man and the serpent are in a life-and-death struggle, and each succeeds in ruining the other – man as he is in God's eyes, and man as he is in his state of disintegrity. The RSV word 'bruise', *shuph*, is difficult to define, but as we see from Job 9: 17, the Hebrew word probably means 'stamp on'. The better MSS of the LXX, however, read it as 'lie in wait for'. Actually no promise is made of any end to the war. That it would appear is a fact of life.

Today we find ourselves questioning the exegesis made by both the Jewish and the Christian interpreters of the early Christian centuries. The Christian idea of a 'proto-evangelium', found in the works of Justin and of Irenaeus, reads like wishful thinking, or as a reading *into* the text what is not there. Irenaeus suggests that it is really Mary the Mother of Jesus who is promised here. The Jewish interpretations in Targ.Ps.-Jon.

and the Jer.Targ. (which are virtually alike) read that 'once men observe the commandments of Torah (the Mosaic Law) they will "direct themselves" to smite you on the head and slay you. But when they neglect the Torah you will "direct yourself" to bite them on the heel. But there is a remedy for the sons of the woman; but for you, serpent, there will be no remedy. They will make peace in the end, in the days of King Messiah.' The Vulgate, again (A.D. 400), the official Latin version of the Bible used by the Western Church for centuries, read '*She* (evidently with reference to Mary) shall bruise thy head, and thou shalt lay snares for (her, his, its) heel'.

16 The second Word of God, describing the factual position of the female of the human species in any unredeemed society, is not a threat but is rather a description of the situation in which woman actually finds herself. In both cases the verb is as much a present tense as it is a future. First, it is she who knows the pain of childbirth, not he. Pregnancy results from her sexual desire for the male. Second, the male in every culture has largely dominated the woman sexually. Even the passionate intercourse of true love can lead to pain. 'Pain', says Bonhoeffer, 'is inherent in the new world of passionate love.' And so it is that in fact in human experience joy and pain are intertwined. So under no circumstances must the woman for this reason turn from the blessing of fertility which God has given to the world; Lev. 26: 9; Jer. 3: 16; Ezek. 36: 11.

17–19 God's Word to the man again is a description of the situation as it is. Man has rejected God's gracious plan for him, that he should live in fellowship with God, in fellowship with his wife, and in harmony with all nature. That total unity of heart and mind has now gone. Man must fight *against* nature and win his daily bread through blood and tears. Man was made to rule the earth, 1: 28; in reality the earth is now ruling him. In the garden, work should have been a delight, because it was God's plan that man should be a creator even as he himself is the Creator, 2: 15. Man was meant to progress in the arts and sciences and, we might add, even visit the moon. But the reality is otherwise. In the end man must return to the soil. It is as if God had now made the creation go into reverse. Sin here is pictured as a kind of infectious disease. Man has corrupted his body. His body is of the earth. Therefore the earth is now cor-

rupt. All nature is now corrupt. Nature has become red in tooth
and claw. The garden produces bread, yes, but it has also
become a patch of thorns and thistles. Joy and pain, even here,
are intermingled. Earthquakes and famine are part of the warp
and woof of human existence. Before our eyes there passes in
review the enormity of the misery of the masses of humanity.
And it is all man's fault, not Nature's, that it is so. And, in the
end, *adam* merely returns to *adamah* (see 2: 7). This is not explained as a *punishment* for man's rebellion. That word is never
used. The verse only describes the world and human life as
these really are.

'We have paved Paradise and put in a parking lot', runs the
popular song; but only after we have killed off the dodo and the
moa, and wiped out the cedars of Lebanon, and turned the
Rhine into a sewer and North Africa into a desert. The whole
environmental issue that we recognize today as a problem is the
outcome of man's alienation from the Nature that knows how to
hold its own balance if man would only refrain from interfering.
God gave man power to *rule* Nature. Instead, man has tried to
exploit Nature. He has thought himself as being *above* the earth,
whereas he is only *of* the earth.

Yet there is still hope. The curse, as we shall see at 5: 29, is
not absolute and final. By God's grace, Noah redeems the
ground from the curse that is described here. That element in
the revelation made here is therefore a promise for the future.

20–21   It is at this point, however, that the man again
seizes upon his God-given faculty of naming, and so of showing
creative power over, his wife. Evidently the image of God in
man is not yet wholly effaced. The man calls his wife Eve,
ḥawwah, 'because she has become the mother of all *ḥai*, living'.
Not, we note, the mother of all human beings, but of all that
lives. The animal creation still depends upon the rule of man.
Eve, the human female, is the 'life-giver' par excellence, through
whom the *living* God channels his creative purpose for all that
lives and breathes. At times in biblical thought Eve is integrated with the idea of Mother Earth, e.g. Ps. 139: 13–15;
Ecclus. 40: 1. Thus the J material here, in its own fashion, does
what P does at 2: 4a and at 5: 1. These both show the oneness
of God's plan in the continuity of life that is to be found in the
élan vital of Nature and in the vitality of the human species.

The man now wildly affirms his right to the creative urge within him, despite the reality of the curse under which he lives. But in so doing he acts in rebellion against God. Yet God actually uses his rebellion to his own glory. This reality is further clarified when we remember that to the Hebrew ear the word *hawwah* expresses a pun. For the root meaning of the verb that uses those consonants means also to lie down flat on one's belly, like the serpent. This nuance in the word was first noted by Ibn Ezra (born A.D. 1090 in Spain). This movement pictures an act of obeisance to a superior.

It is now astonishing to read how 'the Lord God', in the full majesty of his title, renders to the human couple grace in return for their act of rebellion. For he takes them even as they are, just as he also takes the pain of Nature. He clothes their nakedness, their emptiness, their state of dis-integrity (see at 3: 7) in kindliness and love. He gives to man rank and dignity once again, for these can be shown only by the wearing of clothes. Beneath their new clothing, however, they are both still naked. But God in an act of grace has given men the means whereby they can take their mind off their sexual self-consciousness, saying, as it were, 'Now, get on with the job which I have called you to do in the world'. 'You may still stand erect and un-selfconscious in my presence.' So where there is life, there is still hope.

22–24 To live for ever is the essence of divinity. That is why God makes sure that man is only to be a finite creature despite the fact that since he knows he is mortal, man still wishes to live for ever. At the centre of the Garden stands the Tree of Life, 2: 9. Consequently God has to banish man from the Garden so as to turn his mind to the *finite* task of cultivating the soil. In naming Eve as 'life-producer' Adam had demonstrated that he wished to grasp at eternal life. It is interesting to note that v. 22 ends as an incomplete sentence for rhetorical effect. Ideally man can build the Tower of Babel, (chapter 11), and climb up to the sky, or lift himself from his state of alienation from God by his own boot-straps. So God has to verify what Adam has already elected to do. God must cut man off, in *fact*, from being able to live without grace. No wonder that the concept of the immortality of the soul is wholly foreign to the Bible.

In the book of Exodus we read that Pharaoh of Egypt hardened his heart against the Word of God spoken by Moses. This deliberate act of Pharaoh continued to the point that Pharaoh's heart became hardened. But after that we discover that God gives him the *coup de grâce*, so to speak, 'God hardened Pharaoh's heart'. God finalized and completed what man had begun of his own free will. That story is about an event in history. Here we have the eternal reality of this relationship between God and militant man, the principle being expressed here pictorially. Man has already decided that life in the Garden is not what he wants, 3: 8–9. So God merely regularizes man's choice. The reason for God's action is clarified in the final picture of the cherubim. Man must not get it into his head that he can turn round and go back into the Garden just whenever he decides to do so. If God were to allow that, then he would be winking at man's act of rebellion. God therefore confirms the word of the serpent that knowing good and evil means death. Death is separation from the Tree of Life, exclusion from the Garden fellowship with God that man might have experienced as the great reality.

The cherubim (*-im* is the plural suffix) in ancient times were guardians of sacred places, their task being to prevent man from invading the holy; 2 Sam. 6: 2; 1 Kings 6: 23; 8: 6; Ezek. 1: 10; Ps. 18: 10. They were conceived as half animal, half human (as were the seraphim, Isa. 6: 2), something like the Sphinx in Egypt. These creatures were not angels. Angels make themselves apparent to men, in both the OT and the NT, in the form of young men. Angels do not have wings. For angels, like men, are in the image of God; and God does not have wings. An angel is a 'mission' from God (as the Hebrew word means), a messenger who is himself the message from God to man. The cherubim and seraphim are human inventions, theological notions of the divine carved in wood and stone. However, God does not reject these weird human conceptions; instead he uses them as his instruments, and makes them serve his purposes. Their task here is to prevent man *at every turn* from returning of his own accord, in his own strength and at his own sweet will, to the majesty of the unspeakable holiness of the LORD GOD.

Man is now in the position that he cannot save himself. He can be rescued therefore only through an act of God himself, for he alone can conquer sin and death. This of is course as it should be. Man is nothing. God is all in all. The whole future of man, therefore, depends utterly and wholly upon the grace of God alone.

CHAPTER 4

THE SNOWBALLING OF EVIL

1   The significance and the effect of human sexuality are now pictured. No longer do we meet with the words 'man' and 'woman'. For human beings each have their own individual identity. So it is of Adam and Eve that we read, in the same sense as we might speak of Robert and Betty. Adam 'knew' Eve. It is not sufficient to say that he 'lay with' her, as does the NEB. The verb certainly includes the idea of sexual intercourse. But it means much more. It suggests a total knowledge, such as a true husband and wife have of each other when they share all things in common, including even their thoughts. It is from that total situation, then, that a baby is born. The following words require detailed attention.

From the rise of the period of critical studies between the mid-nineteenth century and the beginning of the twentieth, the name Cain was regarded as the collective title of the nation known as the Kenites. But as Skinner pointed out as long ago as 1910, this nasty legend reported here about the origin of the Kenites is not likely to be authentic, in that that people was Israel's friend and ally. They were descended, it was believed, from Hobab (also known as Jethro), Moses' father-in-law, Jud. 4: 11. Moreover, this chapter 4 is not meant to be a historical narrative. Nor has the name Cain anything to do either with the word 'spear', which it resembles, or with a spear-maker, that is to say, a smith, as some suggest. It is a noun derived by popular etymology from the verb 'gotten', RSV, that is to say, speaking theologically, it means 'a begotten one'. Then, since here we are dealing neither with legend, nor with myth, nor again with history, but with the revelation of the plan, not of man, but of God, the next phrase declares that the birth of a human child is an act of God, even when it happens outside of paradise, and to 'natural' man.

This verb *q-n-h* is as versatile as is the English verb 'to get'.

So it can mean, in various circumstances, to acquire, to buy, to create, to appropriate. Its vagueness is noticeable in the important description of the birth of Wisdom in Prov. 8. 22. The point of course is that human birth is a mystery, even though it is a natural process. This reality is again emphasized by the next two words, *'eth* and *Jahweh*.

'Eth can be understood in two ways. (1) It can mean 'with'. So the RSV paraphrases 'with the help of Yahweh', as we prefer to spell the name in English. We note incidentally that from this point onwards in the narrative the J material uses YHWH alone for God, without the addition of *Elohim*. (2) But *'eth* is rarely used with the meaning 'with'. This is because there is another and normal word for 'with', viz. *'im*, which would more easily render into English by 'with the help of'. Again, *'im* is used when there might be doubt about the meaning of the phrase in question if *'eth* were to be used. The commonest usage of *'eth* is as the sign of the accusative when the latter is definite. Now, the noun that *'eth* governs here is in fact definite. If taken this second way, the sentence will read: 'I have gotten a man – the Lord!' That is how Martin Luther understood it 450 years ago. The Versions, however, all differ on the translation. Yet the Targ.Ps.-Jon is worth noting with its 'I have gotten a man, the angel of Yahweh'. For *the* angel at Ex. 23: 20 is the *sign*, *'oth*, (virtually the same word as *'eth*) of Yahweh's saving love. We can only suppose that such a translation speaks of the awe and wonder in the heart of the mother when her first baby is placed in her arms. 'Is this baby real?' 'Is this little red, kicking, crying *thing* – divine?', cf. John 16: 21; Ps. 127: 3. Indeed, no event in the life of a married couple brings them back more truly to contemplate the mystery of life than the birth of their first baby. Here then Eve gives a shout of praise. She has fulfilled God's plan for her as a woman: she has *created* a man.

2 Once again we are in the atmosphere of 'The Pilgrim's Progress' with its symbolic names. Cain can mean 'begotten'. Some scholars suppose that Abel derives from the Assyrian *abbi*, son. Maybe it does. But in the Hebrew tongue Abel means 'vanity', the emptiness and meaninglessness spoken of in the book of Ecclesiastes; cf. also Ps. 39: 5–6; 144: 4; Job 7: 16. By her exclamation Eve probably expresses the bitter consciousness that life to the east of the Garden, that is to say, over the edge of the ordered world, is chaos, vanity, emptiness. Living there, where God is not, is just vanity.

3   Yet it is a *there*. The ancient world as J knew it comprised two types of civilization, the one agrarian, the other pastoral. We are shown here that the humanity that makes its living either by the plough or by shepherding flocks is equally aware that even in the land of vanity man needs God. Life *must* have a meaning, man believes, else there is no purpose in remaining alive. Here we meet with no theory of a meal offering or of a sacrificial offering. The sentence merely expresses the reality that all men are religious and deep within their hearts they feel the need to say a spontaneous 'thank you' to some Power. Yet, since this story is primarily about God and not man, we are not required to justify the acts of man, but are meant to discover the loving plan of God as he proceeds with his elective purpose.

6   This verse tells us what *God* means when he asks Cain this question. If God sees that he can make use of one particular man but not of another, of this nation but not of the next one, who are we to cavil at his design? In a moment, moreover, we are given the necessary answer to the question which our human minds want to raise. God knew that Cain would later commit murder and thus be of no value for his plan, for God knows all. God also knew that Abel, the typical good-living young man, would be cut off in his prime before reaching maturity. Abel's fate thus typifies the kind of tragedy that men can never understand. In the story we note how Abel had given the divinity the best that he had, the 'fat bits'. In his turn God had *noted* Abel's action, *sha'ah*; that is to say God had taken full cognizance of it. What we human creatures must learn, however, is that God has chosen to work through the weak, and not necessarily through the strong, the victim, and not always the victor, through the crucified and not the triumphant for no reason except that that is the kind of God he is. There is no human philosophical answer that can offer any alternative to this picture of God that we find here, as it reveals how the election of man is by grace alone, and not by mere fate.

7   God goes on to explain himself. Although man lives in the land of Vanity, he *can* lead a moral life and he *can* be accepted by God. Instead of letting his face *fall* (evidently resentment had twisted his face) Cain could experience the opposite of disappointment. He could receive confidence to *lift up* his face and stand upright in the presence of God: cf. Gen. 32: 20–21; Mal. 1: 9 (in the Hebrew). Cain has yet to learn what man is *for*. Man lives *for* the service of God. Yet we see from this passage that leading the moral life is not the same thing as re-entering the Garden. The whole Bible makes this message explicit. Cain does not know why he is being rejected. The poor man cannot see into his own mind. He would not have understood why the poet Robert Burns needed to exclaim, 'Would that God the gift would gie us, to see ourselves as others see us'. So the judgment expressed at 3: 24 falls on him kindly and gently. God's last word, consequently, at this point is that man does in fact still possess power and authority to rule over even the subtlest member of the animal world.

We have noted before that we are not to speak of love, or hate, or sin as distinctive entities. These entities are always the actions of human beings. God reminds Cain of this now. The sin here is the greedy action of a living being – we are not told of whom, whether of the serpent, or of the demon lying in wait of Akkadian literature (cf. 1 Peter 5: 8) or in later literature of Satan, or even of a fellow human being; cf. Hos. 13: 7–8; Matt. 7: 9–11. Since God speaks to Cain in the form of a question, 'Are you sure you will be able to master it?', he is really giving Cain a gracious warning.

8–9 Now the story becomes particular. It is well-known, of course, that the old AV does not have the words 'Let us go out to the field' that are there in the RSV. They are not present in the Hebrew original. But the Versions have them, the Sam.Pent., the LXX, and the Syriac. Their addition produces a better flow in the narrative. So we continue by noting the truism that Cain breaks with his brother only because he has first broken with God. 'The harbouring of discontent becomes explosive'; and Cain strikes.

Just as this story is not about man, but is a revelation of the nature of God, so it is not about Cain's act of murder. It is about *God's* purposes with a man and his brother. In vv. 8–11 the word 'brother' occurs six times! It is over against this particular emphasis that the worst possible action against one's brother is recorded as a real possibility. The individual in society can be quite helpless without possessing a friend, *rea'*, or a keeper, *shomer*. That is what a friend is *for*. Murders are committed most commonly, not against strangers, but within the family – for within its walls can be the long harbouring of discontent. In the same way civil wars are often the fiercest of all wars. Cain probably did not mean to kill his brother; he just hit harder than he knew. In this way each new generation has to relearn the power of a bad temper, the possible terrible outcome of a little word of slander or malice. But, as God has just said to Cain, man *can* control his temper if he puts his mind to it. Yet how complicated life is. The first murder grew out of an act of worship.

Holzinger has suggested that the word *wayyomer*, 'and (Cain) said' (to Abel), v. 8, might have been originally *wayyishmor*. A change of one letter only in the Hebrew consonantal text would thus give the meaning, 'Cain eyed Abel'; that is to say, Cain lay in wait for Abel his brother. This is an attractive possibility.

As in the case of Adam, 3: 9, so with Cain. God, the Judge of all the earth, does not accuse Cain. We are now standing, it seems, in the divine court of law where no man is considered guilty till he is proved so. And once again God merely asks a question, not 'Where are *you*', as to Adam, but this time 'Where is your *brother*?'

It is horrifying that the word employed by Cain in his reply to God, 'Am I my brother's *shomer*?' can mean one that keeps his eye on his brother. Richardson points out, on the other hand, that the word 'watch over' is often applied to the task of the good shepherd. If this last is the true sense of the active participle which Cain uses, then what we hear from his lips is no less than blasphemy. For Cain is here addressing the Good Shepherd himself! In this way, then, Cain rejects the revealed will of God for man, viz., that a man is *responsible* for his neighbour. When Cain says 'I don't know', his sin has become part of his total mode of life. His 'I' in the Hebrew original, we might add, is the emphatic of sheer egotism.

10   The divine Judge is, however, unshaken. He remains true to himself, as Ezekiel constantly declares; and so he does not act in anger in response to man's insolence. He continues the trial unruffled. He asks another question, this time one in

which he states the case for the indictment. The 'cry' from the ground is the word that is found at Ex. 3: 7, where Israel cries to God from Egypt; it is the word used for the cry for legal protection that is God's great concern to give. Both the blood and the life belong to God. To murder another therefore is to attack God's own possession. The Hebrew might possibly mean 'Hark! Your brother's blood . . .' as if Abel were still alive and calling from below the ground; cf. Job 16: 18. If we declare that Cain thought he had put an end to his brother simply by shedding his blood, whereas in reality his blood was now shouting to high heaven, what we are doing is to pictorialize the theological truth that the murder has shown its eschatological significance; cf. 1 John 3: 2. As we noted, God is on the side of the poor, the outcast, and especially the victims of violence. Rev. 6: 9 pictures such as closest to God's heart by showing them preserved under God's altar. And again, as we have noted, such are the true elect of God, not those who rule by force of arms. God is thus both their Judge and their Advocate at the same time. Indeed, the cry of the murdered goes up *unto me*. In consequence of this, as C. Westermann admits wryly, there can be no perfect murder!

11–12   The Judge pronounces his verdict. Since *adam* has impregnated the *adamah* with human life-blood, as if it were his semen, *adam* can no longer be one in essence with Sister Earth. He is to be isolated *away from*, *min*, her. This condition is the opposite of being in *shalom* with it, that is, integrated with it. At 3: 17 it was said that the ground now bore God's condemnation, so that man could live off it only by toil and sweat. The situation is now worse; the soil, the basis of man's very existence, is now at variance with man. It is as if it had become physically infected by a virus; cf. Lev. 18: 25. Sister Earth, with her dust-bowls, and earthquakes, and floods and ice-ages, has now become man's enemy. She is monstrous; she is Rahab, drunk with the blood of Abel. So she militates against true growth, turning agricultural land into desolation, the haunt of demons and vampires, Isa. 13: 18–22; 24: 4–13; 34: 8–15. Thus, from this point on we cannot speak again of Mother Earth; for Earth is now man's Sister through the blood of Abel. Anyone who today has walked over a battlefield knows exactly what J means, when he gazes upon good ground sown with spent shrapnel like dragon's teeth, forests burnt with napalm, devastated villages, sunken vessels. But more, tribal feuds will now be the norm. The words, 'Here's a stranger, let's kill him', will resound wherever wandering refugees should find themselves. Cain will dwell *away from* the security of land, family life, kith and kin, and from blood-relationship, the unity brought about by a common religious tradition. The words, 'vagrant and vagabond', that interesting pair of alliterative words that occur here in the Hebrew, are thus a real picture of man no longer at peace with the soil from which he was taken. So the Fall of man has both cosmic and eschatological significance. Yet this general theological statement can be expressed only in the form of the particular, in the same way that Jesus could only speak of the End in terms of the destruction of the city of Jerusalem, Matt. 24.

13–14   Man has always whined at his fate. How often does he exclaim, 'If I were God, I would do so and so'. By just throwing out such a criticism of events man reveals his titanism and rebellion against the very notion that God may after all have a comprehensive plan in view. And so the little addition 'and from thy face I shall be hidden' is merely a pious fraud, in that man has already hidden himself from God, 3: 9, not God from man. Of course Cain's exclamation is based upon the ancient view that a god had jurisdiction over only a particular territory and over the life of only one nation. And yet we are to see that God does, at will, withdraw his protection from a man or nation and may indeed abandon him to the natural course of events, Deut. 31: 17.

It is not that Cain feels remorse. How true a picture this is of the hardened criminal type. The word '*awon* means first 'sin' (in the sense of acting from a twisted nature), and then second, it means being aware of what the sin entails, viz. 'punishment'. The Targum misses the point in translating 'My iniquity is too great to be pardoned'; but it may be excused in that the verb 'to bear' can also mean 'to be forgiven'. For only when Cain has eventually developed a conscience does he begin to see his act as a sin, and sin, not only in the sight of God, but in the eyes of *all men*. In other words, Cain has now discovered that he is the 'Prodigal Son' amongst sycophants and prostitutes, in a country far from God.

15   God at once corrects the pagan notion that man can escape from God. The text runs 'Not so' in the RSV. This is the Hebrew *lachen*, a word that can be used to solemnly introduce a covenant promise. No matter to where Cain wanders, he will find God there, already there, in the fulness of his grace and mercy, and forgiving love. Under no circumstances was anyone to lay hands on Cain. For Yahweh's 'face' protects a man from revenge even in a blood feud. The number 'sevenfold' is to occur later at 4: 24. We are to keep it in mind as the number God himself chooses, for it is to be the key to other matters.

We are now to see what looks to us as an intolerable judgment. But it is couched in that form of semitic vividness such as Jesus used when he said, 'If your right eye offend you, pluck it out'. It is as a kind of brake upon the awful judgment that God puts this mark upon Cain. The word 'mark' is a very potent noun. It means both a sign and a symbol of what the mere mark itself indicates, much as a wedding ring means more than that it is made of gold. This mark is evidently a sign of the grace and loving concern of God for sinners. So we see that Cain does not have the last word. It is God who does. Incidentally we note that it is only a perverted exegesis that regards the mark of Cain as the curse of God upon one section of the human race.

The important issue before us is that the biblical God who loves to make covenants here makes the first of all his many covenants. While not named as such (we shall meet with the word for the first time in chapter 6), God's action bears the mark of the covenant upon it. And what we find to be so very astonishing is that God's first covenant is made with a sinner. It is not that the ordinary man is an 'atheist'; it is not that he denies the existence of God. He is just living in separation from God, whom he thinks of as being 'up in heaven' while he is on earth. So God has to make man aware of his need of God. This human awareness of being 'away from home' is expressed here acutely. At 4: 14 Cain had said that he would be a fugitive and a wanderer. This word wanderer is now affirmed. Cain must now dwell in the 'land of Nod'. But Nod is merely the Hebrew for 'wandering'. So we are made aware of the paradox of human life, in that man seeks to remain, to reside, in the land of wandering! Although he is on the move through time, in order to find security he 'digs in' as we say and puts his trust in those things that money can buy. We notice that living in this land of wandering is a continuation of the experience of the chaos that is not order, for this land too lies 'east of Eden', or perhaps 'confronting Eden', as an aggressive challenge to all that Eden stands for. Thus we are not far from the truth when we say that the basic sociological problem of man is really theological!

17–22   The paradox goes farther. We hear of man, not just settling in, but actually building a city in the land of Nod! It is as if he built a house on a sandbank where the river may rise at any time instead of upon a rock. Who built the city?, we may ask. Was it Cain or was it Enoch? And who was Cain's wife? These questions need never arise if we but remember that we are 'seeing' revelation in pictures, in the style of the Pilgrim's Progress and not reading literal history. Yet there can be an overtone of incipient historicism here. Included in the general revelation about the uprooted nature of man and about man's struggle to establish himself apart from God it is possible that the historical people, the Kenites (despite what we said at 4: 1!) are also referred to here as a particular instance of the general rule. The Kenites had from time immemorial been a wandering nomadic tribe. But with the development of civilization, they, like some other nations, were gradually sucked into an urban way of life. This was an issue known to J at the time of writing in the days of King Solomon.

We do not know either the symbolic or the literal meaning of all the names that follow. Two of them contain the word EL, 'God'. Enoch, for example, may mean 'consecrated', 'dedicated', so-called in connexion with the founding of a city. The ancient world was naturally religious. So this city was dedicated to all that is the opposite of the joy and the peace of Eden. Mehujael may mean 'God gives life'; others suggest the opposite, 'God blots out', thus bringing the curse to its ultimate conclusion. And Methushael may mean either 'God's man' or 'Man of the netherworld'. Irad may mean 'He who flees, or as some suggest 'a wild ass'. It is a common feature of traditions that names should rhyme when their meanings are not immediately apparent; for rhyme helps the memory to retain a long list of names. Enoch here is not the same Enoch whom we meet at 5: 18–24. What we are to note, however, is that Cain, the violent sinner, yet under God's protection, has become the father of human civilization. Man *can* build a civilization, it seems. Man *can* raise himself from the hovel to the ceiled house, and he *can* even produce an ordered society out of chaos; cf. Luke 16: 8. But he can raise himself up only to the level of man, not to that of God.

Lamech has no need of God. In consequence his life is a steady descent into chaos. He rejects the law of God that alone creates complete harmony and love, 2: 22–24, and takes to himself two wives. The popular saying that 'marriages are made in heaven' Lamech would have swept aside with contempt. The name Adah means something like 'adornment', evidently suggesting a superficial and 'phoney' personality. Zillah means 'shadow'. The second wife was a mere nonentity. In monogamy there is a union of interest and of work; the couple can battle together against the slings and arrows of outrageous fortune. But when a man has two wives, or up to four as in Islam, he approaches each of his women as merely his private property and even the object of his lust. In the case of monogamy life together becomes a vocation; in polygamy self-interest is on the throne. Yet, J declares that the various branches of civilized life are in fact maintained and furthered by man in his self-interested drive to succeed.

23–24 Jabal and Jubal are 'brothers'. This means that J believes that animal culture and the art of the musician are essentially ancient. So while both these aspects of civilization belong within man's creative drive, man's moral declension proceeds to avalanche towards moral chaos. It may well be that J introduced these lines of verse to his narrative in that they were already known to the Israel of his day. For they are in the style of the taunt-song, the Arabian *Hija* or battle-satire that goes back to Israel's very early period. The verse says something decisively revealing about human nature. At 4: 15 we learned that God forbids a slaying for a slaying. Vengeance is his, and his alone, even to sevenfold. Man never has the necessary knowledge of the facts to give tit-for-tat. Lamech, however, takes the divine right of sevenfold revenge to himself, and then multiplies it to seventyfold. Consequently, in the violence of his lust to kill, Lamech even rejects the divine protection offered to Cain. Lamech insists upon his own mastery of the situation. He will be 'the captain of his soul'. He will even dare God to damn him for being a 'he-man'.

That this is no mere description of pre-historic man comes home to us concretely in our own day and generation. From country after country we read of reports such as this: 'If you shoot the ten hostages you have taken, we will shoot the hundred we have taken'. This poem is thus a revelation of the heart of natural man, such as he is at all times; cf. Jud. 16: 28; 2 Sam. 21: 1–9. Before the word 'I have slain' lies the particle *ki*; in this case it follows an unspoken oath. So we can understand the wild shout to be 'I swore to kill a man just for (let us say) giving me a black eye, a young lad just for touching me' (one meaning of the verb). The two lines, however, form a hendiadys, and thus refer to the one incident in poetic parallelism. Lamech's blasphemous oath is but his way of taking in vain the divine dictum that we heard uttered at 4: 15. There it occurs in the passive voice. This is a Hebrew device to show the immutability of the declaration.

There are those today who speak of 'the fierce Old Testament Law' and decry as pagan the Lex Talionis that we find at Ex. 21: 23–25, the law of 'an eye for an eye, a tooth for a tooth'. What such critics do not realize is that the introduction of this 'law of the talon' is an astounding achievement in the history of man. So far it has not as yet been outdated in these so-called advanced and civilized days of ours, as we noted above, in that natural man has not climbed up even yet to the level of this three-thousand-year-old law. The real climbing up to the divine level is what Jesus refers to when he bids us, neither to take vengeance seventy-sevenfold, nor to demand an eye for an eye, but rather to forgive our enemy seventy times seven, Matt. 18: 22.

Up to this point this chapter has provided us with a theological statement about the nature of evil and has declared how, in proportion as men multiply, so does evil snowball in the world. Yet since all creation is one, the evil that is there in the 'high places' (as we shall see later at 6: 1–4) is of a piece with the evil in the heart of man, 6: 5. This chapter therefore guides us to understand how it is that the nature of Satan develops and snowballs until it becomes the wholly evil thing that we find in the New Testament. The word *satan* is used in the early books of the OT to mean merely a human adversary, personal or national, Num. 22: 32; 1 Sam. 29: 4. The figure of *the* Adversary appears only three times in the OT, at Job 1–2, Zech. 3: 1–3, and at 1 Chron. 21: 1. In those three instances he is regarded as an 'angel', and as doing the bidding of God; but in the last two instances he seems to be relishing his task unnecessarily. In the NT, however, Satan has now become 'the very Devil'. Evidently, it would appear, with the entrance into the world of him whom the NT claims to be the pure Light of Gen. 1: 3, evil hits back in the form of total Darkness. However, since evil can be conceived only in terms of human activity, Satan is finally given the comprehensive title of the Prince of Darkness.

25–26   Life goes on. The life force is something that God has blessed, 1: 28. ' "She" called his name Substitute.' The purpose of God now in motion cannot be thwarted, even by death. The 'she' continues to say, '(I swear) that God has substituted (or appointed) for me another seed'. From this substitutionary line there derives a new line of human beings, for Enosh is just another word for man or Adam.

The root of this name means to be weak or gentle or humble, that is to say, not violent or vicious. The noun occurs in Psalm 8, where the thoughtful, overawed speaker, as he gazes at the heavens, exclaims, 'What is *enosh*, that thou art mindful of him?'; but immediately in poetic parallelism he continues with 'and descendants of Adam, that thou dost care for them?' (for both words for 'man' are collective), and of course Enosh is still the sons of Adam.

'At that time men began to call upon the name of the Lord' – a grand affirmation. It tells us that while the great civilizations of man developed in might, in economic strength, and in intellectual and artistic attainment, right in their midst there were to be found people who named Yahweh as their God. Or, as we would prefer to say, people who called upon the living God whom Israel later on called Yahweh. Although this is what Israel did in faraway Babylonia in the sixth century, Isa. 44: 5, there is no suggestion here that this new line of believers is meant to refer to Israel. What we read is, 'Then it was begun to call . . .'. The statement means that there have always been men of humble heart in every land and in every civilization, people who have lived in dependency upon their divinity, whatever name they have known him by.

Enosh is therefore true man rather than Adam, on the ground that he calls upon God, and in doing so keeps remembering his likeness to God; cf. Ex. 33: 19. But this one short verse is sufficient to awaken the Christian never to say in antisemitic arrogance that the Church was born at Pentecost. For it has always been upon such dependence and affirmation of the divine Name that God has built his church; cf. Deut. 6: 4; Matt. 16: 16–18. Here then we discover a worshipping community, in that the phrase 'to call upon the Lord' is a technical expression for an organized cult (S. H. Hooke). Finally we perceive here that the People of God, of whatever composition, is no religio-political theocracy. Its role is solely a spiritual diakonia.

This chapter, then, suggests that man has the choice of living at three levels, the sensual, the creative, and the trusting.

CHAPTER 5

THE GENERATIONS OF ADAM

1   That this chapter is a continuation of P's material in chapter 1 is explicitly declared by the device used in v. 1. P's first material ended at 2: 4a with the words 'These are the generations . . .'. Chapter 5 begins with a similar phrase. This ancient method of showing continuity of authorship is observable elsewhere. For example, the last two verses of 2 Chron. are identical with the first two verses of Ezra.

P has already told us about the 'generations of the heavens and the earth'. Now he shows his interest in listing this time ten generations of mankind. These stretch in this chapter from Adam to Noah. Moreover P agrees without comment with what J has to say on this matter in chapters 3–4, viz. that, despite man's sinfulness, the divine image has in fact been transmitted from generation to generation, 5: 1, 3; 9: 6. This means that the two sources agree to state that the divine image in man has only been defaced, not obliterated. The blessing of God uttered at 1: 26–31 is thus still valid. It could not be otherwise. For God never goes back on his word. In fact man's continuing fruitfulness actually marks the working-out of the blessing. We find therefore that each new-born son is a new being in his own right, even a new creation. Here then P gives us a list of *people*, each person being different from the other.

'Humanity' is a concept unknown to the ancient world, just as is the idea of 'society' of which we speak so much today. We do not find 'humanity' here in this chapter. Rather we hear of the first male and female *persons* whom *together* God himself, not we, named Adam, v. 2. Yet people do form one humanity, and together they are in the image of God. C. Westermann declares that the J genealogies (which we met in chapter 4) vary considerably in form within themselves. In P, he says, on the other hand, they are constant and strictly stylized; P uses them, he says, as a scaffolding for what some scholars call his *Urgeschichte*

(Primal i.e. – not formal – History) to lead up eventually to the Patriarchs. So he is concerned to trace the redemptive plan of God in its first stages. J is more interested to show that the crafts arise from God's gifts of various abilities, so that man's culture and the separation of mankind into the various nations is of God.

Just as the first period of creation produced a rhythm of night and day, so in this second part we meet with the rhythm of life and death, and death as the inevitable accompaniment of life. How often do we read: 'And he died . . .', v. 5, 8, 11, etc. Yet that the people named here can live extraordinarily lengthy lives is the emphasis made. Life is God's gift, yet those who live in God's plan must not hide from death nor pretend that it is not there.

The theory was long held that the figures found in this chapter were adapted by P from the numbers found in the lists of the early Babylonian kings. We know of this list of ten kings from the Greek historian, Berossus, though he flourished long after the period reached by the spade of the modern archaeologist. The last king in this Babylonian list, interestingly enough, was saved, like Noah, from the Great Flood reported in the historical myths of the peoples of Mesopotamia. Scholars have supposed that P used the numbers he found in these old lists to produce a schema by which he was enabled to count backwards from the biblical Flood to the Creation of man. The meaning of the high numbers before us, however, seems to have been lost even by the sixth century B.C., when the chapter was compiled. Certainly this was so a few centuries later, because both the LXX and the Sam.Pent. differ greatly from the Hebrew text in the matter of the numbers they give us. The total span of time that we meet with here in the MT is 1656 years. But the Sam.-Pent. makes it 1307 years, and the LXX 2242 years! However, this Babylonian explanation of the curious numbers has today been largely abandoned. For we have now discovered that the genealogy which P uses may actually be older even than the Babylonian list of kings. And anyway, the Babylonians counted 432,000 years from the Creation to the Flood! Moreover, the text of chapter 5, as we have it in the MT, seems to contain a combination of what we have already met in J, at 4: 25–26 and at 4: 17–18 with some names now found in the book of

Chronicles. However that may be, there is a very important emphasis made by the list. Since Adam is not meant to be a historical character, his long life may well represent a theological picture of the potency of the blessing of God, just as the 'far country' in the story of the Prodigal Son is a theological picture of the state of mind of the younger son in question, and certainly not a place on the map, Luke 15: 13. So what we have is P's way of declaring that in ancient times the world began to fill up with people by the will of God. The length of the lives of these antediluvian characters thereupon progressively shortens in proportion as the world fills up.

We may put this explanation of the long lives of these old heroes in still another way. An author might decide to write a book about chivalry. But chivalry is an abstract idea, and so is not an attractive topic for a book. Our author accordingly decides to let the concepts of medieval chivalry reveal themselves by the method of recounting the acts of King Arthur and his Knights of the Round Table. No matter that we cannot establish the historicity of Arthur. He may even be a mythical character. What matters is the description of what chivalry is. The author merely uses the stories of the Knights as a framework upon which to hang the description he wishes to give us. In the same way, P is not concerned either about the historicity of his antediluvians or about the length of their days on earth. He uses them merely as a framework for his theology. Thus there is no need for concern when we discover that the long life of some of these personages means that they actually survived the Flood!

In the whole Priestly material in the OT this love of genealogies is prominent. It is an interest carried on into the books of Chronicles and then into the NT, where Matthew and Luke each give us a genealogy of Jesus that makes use of P's material. What is important is not the accuracy of these lists – for that would be difficult to maintain in some cases. What matters is why the lists are there at all. It is because they reveal a view of history that is unique to Israel in the ancient world. These lists of 'begats' are actually declaring that history is to be understood as a progression along a human line throughout the centuries. The OT is the only literature from out of the whole ancient world that makes such a declaration; moreover, all modern views on the meaning of history derive from it. History, says P, has a beginning, a middle, and an end. Moreover, man in his generations is the vehicle of the divine purpose which keeps pressing on towards a goal.

The Babylonians, the Canaanites, and the rest of Israel's neighbours held no such view of history. Each generation of man in their view of the passage of time was unrelated to past and future, and a new period would begin simply with the reign of a new king. For example, we do not know from the book of Exodus either who was the Pharaoh of the oppression or who was the Pharaoh of the crossing of the Sea. Each is known simply as 'Pharaoh'. For 'Pharaoh' was the timeless incarnation of the Sun-God. In the story of Israel, however, which we read in the book of Exodus, we discover the meaning of time and of the significance of its passing; e.g. Ex 7: 25; 12: 2, 40; 19: 1; 23: 10; 40: 17. Later on in history the Greeks did in fact develop the art of history writing. Thus Thucydides could tell the story of the Peloponnesian war in great detail, even showing cause and effect as the story proceeds. But the Greeks never became historians in the true sense. Rather they were reporters, as Toynbee declares, and good ones at that. This was because they could not see where events were leading to; they were never able to show any meaning or purpose running through the story they had to tell. Not possessing a God who is *outside* of history, and who is guiding all history to *his* ultimate goal, all they could do was to describe the events they experienced over a limited period. What is more, the Greeks learned from the Egyptians the idea that history moves in great cycles covering several centuries at a time. But P sees history as running in a straight line and leading to a goal. Even the Marxist today has taken his philosophy of history from the OT, and looks for the 'end' of history in what he believes will be the perfect society. On the other hand, in the OT men may either co-operate in or equally defy God's plan to bring all things to their ultimate goal. It makes no difference to God in the end. For example, events in the very long reign of Jeroboam II, 2 Kings 14: 23–27, are dismissed in but a few lines, because 'he did what was evil in the sight of the Lord'. That is to say, Jeroboam did not submit to be used by God in his day and generation. The plan of God goes forward, however, in Jeroboam's son, Hezekiah, even though a whole generation of movement toward the goal has been lost. So that is why the writer sees no point in telling us what happened during those 'lost' years.

P begins his story where J ends his, by continuing the line from Adam with the latter's son, Seth, 4: 26. He thus passes by the line that leads up to Lamech. This means that he is just as concerned as is J to emphasize that the People of God – in whatever way we may name Seth's descendants in later centuries – have their beginning 'in the beginning'. This theme is renewed at 11: 10–26. P's material is primarily the story of election. We read at 1: 4 that in creating Nature God had 'made a separation'. In the book of Exodus, too, we read that God 'made a separation' between Israel and 'all other people that are on the face of the earth', Ex. 33: 16. Here then this basic principle within God's plan is expressed again. Both J and P declare that God has elected one of the lines descending from Adam and has made special use of that line for his plan and purpose. This does not mean that God has rejected those listed in 4: 17–23. For not to be used does not mean either to be rejected or to be damned. What this passage does portray is the sovereign grace of God in action, as he chooses whom he wills for the purpose he has in mind. We note therefore that if Kenan, v. 9, is the same person as Cain (for this might embody an alternative spelling) then God has indeed accepted Cain, sinner as he is, even though he did not accept his offering, 4: 5, and uses him for his plan.

18   Without warning and well down the list, we meet with the name of Enoch – is he the Enoch who was son of Cain? We even receive some information about him apart from the length of his days on earth. His years are 365, evidently a reference to what the ancient world noted was a solar year. Are we being told by this meaningful figure that Enoch lived through an ordinary cycle of human life and so is not to be regarded as some kind of superman? We cannot say for sure. However that may be, P tells us plainly that 'Enoch walked with God' throughout most of his days. This must mean that Enoch did not merely *believe* that God existed. Nor is P saying that Enoch believed *in* God. This last phrase smacks too much of a human resolve, making faith into a kind of 'works'. His phrase is simple, that Enoch just *walked* with God. The verb to walk with God means 'to conduct one's life in God's ways'. *Tor*. Should this Enoch after all be the Enoch whom J mentions at 4: 17 (and P would inherit J's material as it came down to him over the generations), then P is telling us that God can elect even him who builds a city in the land of wandering, and that despite Lamech's wild oath to be avenged 77 times, 4: 24, God allows his son to live 777 years, 5: 31. Enoch, it seems, just accepted quite simply God's prevenient grace, and then lived his life along with God. Since Enoch is no more an historical character than is the Prodigal Son, we see that P uses his name here to reveal that at any time and in any place it is possible for man, as Micah 6: 8 puts it, 'to walk humbly with your God', although the verbs in Hebrew are not the same. We note that Micah addresses *man*, Adam, in this passage, not Israelite man, far less Christian man! The phrase occurs again at 6: 9, where we are told that Noah, the man in whom God's plan of redemption 'rested', also walked with God.

After this phrase, P continues with, 'and he was not, for God took him'. The implication is the same as that used by Jesus when he refuted a group of Sadducees 'who say there is no resurrection', Mark 12: 18. Jesus answers their argument with the divine logic which God used when speaking to Moses: 'I am the God of Abraham, Isaac and Jacob' (these his ancestors lived and died several centuries before Moses). That is to say, God is not the God of the dead but of the living. Since the God of Enoch, according to P, is the living God, then Enoch must still be alive with God. It is natural that Enoch later became the subject of much legend; cf. the works 'The Assumption of Enoch', 'The Book of Enoch', etc.

A final point to note is that in the OT there is no discussion of the mystery of death. No one asks the senseless question, 'Do you believe in life after death?' For there is no such thing as life apart from God. Instead, as here, the basic question is seen to be, 'Do you walk with God, now?' All that follows from that question rests with God, not man; cf. Ps. 49: 15; 91: 16.

28   Such is the elective purpose of God that a believing son may spring from an evil father, as we see in the genealogies of Jesus, some of whose ancestors were highly questionable characters. Faith, in other words, is not necessarily an inherited commodity. Moreover, cruel Lamech makes a 'prophetic' utterance about his son Noah that we find fulfilled in chapter 9. It seems that the promises of God may issue from the mouths, not only of saints, but of sinners.

29 The name Noah, etymologically speaking, derives from one of two possible Hebrew roots, one meaning 'comfort', the other 'rest'. Quite probably, however, to those who heard the name in Hebrew both meanings presented themselves at once. At 6: 6 we shall see that God 'comforted himself' about the whole issue of creating man, when God 'rested' in Noah and in his Ark. The verb is, of course, used pictorially. The writer's genius then is to offer us two theologies from this one story. This may be illustrated by the manner in which God's use of Jonah is developed in two ways in the NT, at Matt. 12: 39, 41, and 39: 40.

32 Noah has three sons. We can see from v. 29 that God is going to use them in some special way. From the name Shem we moderns have created the name Semite. Ham means 'hot', and came to be used to cover the peoples of the hot south, especially along the Upper Nile. Japheth (we shall examine the meaning of the name at 9: 27) came to be regarded as the ancestor of the Canaanites and their neighbours. Without seeking to be accurate in this regard, what P is telling us is that through Noah and his family all the peoples of the Near East (the known world of his day) are to receive the blessing of God. In other words, God in his patience and mercy delays the necessary judgment for ten long generations yet, before he finally acts.

CHAPTER 6

GOD'S JUDGEMENT ON SIN

1–4   The first four verses of chapter 6 have intrigued interpreters all down the centuries. They appear to derive from a
new source altogether. Some scholars use the geological term
'erratic boulder' to describe them – that is a rock which a glacier
has carried far from its source and has then dropped. The
passage, which may in fact be composite, is an example, *par
excellence*, of the genre we named in the Introduction. It is most
truly 'theology in pictures'; for even the biblical literalist would
have difficulty in taking these verses at their face value. Yet this
passage, which the final editor has incorporated at this point, is
of deep significance in the area of meaning and reality. In a
word, what is 'revealed' to us here is that evil is not confined to
the human heart, but is part and parcel of the woof and web of
the universe in which man dwells. In the area 'between heaven
and earth' titanic insolence is to be found just as much as in
human life; naturally this reality is expressible only in the
language of myth.

We meet here with the general myth of the Titans, such as
was familiar to the Greeks, a race conceived as being half gods,
half men. Before Israel arrived in Canaan some of its inhabi-
tants had clearly been a tall race. For example, Josh. 12: 4
speaks of Og, 'one of the remnant of the giants'. These were
known variously as *Nephilim, Emim, Anakim, Rephaim, Zam-
zummim*. The semi-mythological nature of these mighty men is
represented particularly in the name *Rephaim*, which can also
mean ghosts or shades of the dead. Despite their being 'half-caste
gods', the descendants of those lusty giants remained wholly
non-divine. Even the semi-divine pagan kings of the ancient
world went down into Sheol when they died, Ezek. 32: 27.
Thus although the Egyptian Pharaohs were all depicted as
giants, they too were buried in human tombs. Another meaning
for the name *Nephilim* might be 'dropped ones', in that they

were they results of miscarriages, or again this word may suggest the idea of Mongols resulting from unnatural unions. Clearly we are warned not to meddle with genetic mutations in man in order to seek to create the giant, the perfect man. Since the meddlers with the process are all titans themselves, they must recognize that their aims will end, not as they had hoped, but in the tomb that all humanity must meet. Nor are we meant to think, as did the Greeks, that 'there were giants in the land in those days'. For we are meant, not to look back, but to live in the present and with hope for the future.

These 'sons of God' *saw* that human girls were 'good'. This is the use of the word we met in chapter 1. The girls were good for them to rape. They came, they *saw*, they conquered, so to speak. As Westermann puts it, 'The lusty shall inherit the earth'. And so we think of the ceaseless waves of human conquest, by Huns, Goths, Vandals, Mongols, and all the rest. We have to be aware of this reality about the lusty conqueror if we are to understand why God reacts to this total titanism in his chosen manner. God had created 'the heavens and the earth' as *one*. Such 'holism' requires a whole action from the *only* God.

It was sufficiently hinted at in the episode of the Garden that the man–woman relationship which is completed through sex is man's Achilles' heel. If sexual desire is allowed to dominate a man's motives, then a door into every area of his personality is pushed open, and he becomes so titanic in his lust for both domination and power that he is ready to destroy those who stand in his way. Thus a right attitude to sex is not a social, much less a personal issue, but a theological one. Right throughout the OT lust is denounced as the basic destructive agency in human life. For example, Prov. 7: 6–27 states the general principle, that lust leads to the death of the human spirit, as do such passages as Gen. 34: 7; Lev. 18; 2 Sam. 12: 9 and 13: 12, along with Hosea 4: 12–14.

The longevity of the heroes listed in chapter 5 explains, as we have seen, the population explosion that followed. But even as man multiplied so did his titanism. God has therefore to limit the evil that man can do to a span of 120 years. Man lives, anyway, only because God has put his own spirit, his breath, in him. On the other hand God has decreed that there is no such thing as natural immortality, or immortality of the 'soul'. This indeed is *revelation*, in contradistinction to the *religious ideas* of natural man, to be found particularly in the religions of the East. When the greatest hero in Israel's story, Moses, reached this outer boundary of 120 years, even he *died*.

The meaning of the first verb in v. 3 is doubtful. It may mean, 'My spirit shall not *abide* [permanently, LXX] in man for ever'; or again, 'will not shield man for ever', *Tor*; or, 'strive with' him, AV. The Targum reads, 'be humbled in'. If the last is correct, the writer is saying that God sets a limit to man's insolence. But von Rad suggests that the verb is from a root meaning 'rule', so that he would translate by 'punish'. The inference is then that God is immediately on the spot with his Word, in this case very much the Word of judgment. Even this 'erratic boulder', then, does not offer us first of all information about man. Rather, with the rest of these eleven chapters, it reveals to us first of all the Word of God.

They had sought to be 'men of renown' by means of their sexual potency; not that their permissive ways is all that is meant by the phrase. For in the story found at 11: 1–9 we discover that the purpose that men have in building the 'tower of Babel' is in order to storm the heavens. As we have said, however, sexual licence is commonly the first step towards the destruction of the image of God in man. This is an element in this 'revelatory' passage of which modern, Western man is ignorant indeed. God had blessed man's sexual powers, chapter 1, for they were to be used in obedience to his plan for the world. Man, however, has made a god out of one of God's creatures; man worships the Tree of Life itself. This is a breaking of the First Commandment. That is why that Commandment is the first to be stated.

5–7   God's *seeing* is often the introduction to a narrative that follows. It means the discovery, the showing up, the revelation, of a situation *as it is*. Seeing means more than noticing. When God sees, then action always follows. The action begins by a Word. It is, as Frey puts it, God's unnerving No to Man's daemonism and titanism. Since God does not exist for himself, but for man, it is no wonder that God feels the pain which man causes him, Hos. 11: 8–9.

The word 'wickedness', RSV, is not to be understood as 'sin'. It is really the word 'evil'. Evil is now depicted as at its ground swell. Evil is at man's roots. Even man's plans are evil, for the imagination of man's heart is evil from his youth', 8: 21. This word 'imagination' means the *bent* of a man's heart. But this v. 5 is a blanket expression to cover the totality of evil which shows itself in natural man, an awareness known both to Jeremiah, Jer. 17: 9, and to Jesus, Matt. 15: 19. Evil is the evidence of a kind of schizophrenia in both man and nature. God is one. He has created his universe as one *uni*-verse. He has made each man to be one whole unified person. The licentiousness of the Canaanites against which the Mosaic Law warns the people of God marks the first step in this splitting up of the human personality. In 842 B.C. Queen Jezebel sought to impose Baal-worship upon the northern kingdom, Israel. The god Baal was the apotheosis of male virility, and his consort, Astarte, was the deification of female fecundity. As we learn from the work of Hosea, a century later than Queen Jezebel, you deify the miracle of the life-process only because you are controlled by the spirit of lust. For sex as an end in itself serves only part of a man. It is no longer, in lust, the instrument of the whole integrated person that lives in harmony with himself, with his neighbour, and with God; for it is not now controlled by obedience to the mind of God. The tragedy of the situation is that man is unaware of his own schizophrenic nature. As the Russian writer Solzhenitsyn describes this reality in his *The Gulag Archipelago*, II, 'In ordinary human societies the human being lives out his sixty years without ever getting caught in the pincers [of the betrayal of one's own kin in the forced labour camps], and he himself is quite convinced of his decency, as are those who pronounce speeches over his grave. A human being departs from life without ever having learned into what kind of deep well of evil one can fall!' So much for Nietzschian man; evil can kill even his human spirit.

The God of the Bible is known as the *living* God. Thus he experiences in his own 'heart' what we living men and women, made in his image, experience in our own hearts. Such a view is very different from the theology of the epic poems of the Near East which provide the framework, the structure, for what follows. In them we have a conflict *between the gods*. Here we have a conflict *within the one God*. 'And the Lord was sorry. . . .'

The action revealed by this last verb is pictured at 8: 21,

where God himself declares that he has changed his plan. So it would seem that God is not unchangeable, immutable, passionless, nor is he the *kismet,* of Muslim thinking, to be understood in terms of the popular song 'Che sarà, sarà'. He is the God who displays a loving, creative purpose. This means that if the particular road he has travelled with man, even as man travels on in his freedom, happens to end in an impasse, then God in *his* freedom is ready to make a change. So here we enter upon a new OT *Gattung,* type, or genre of writing, one that had been fully exemplified in the poem in Deut. 32 before ever J 'put pen to paper'. It might be named the Guilt-Punishment-Rescue *Gattung;* and it becomes basic to the whole biblical revelation. For by its use we see the expression of God's total judgment in response to humanity's total rebellion. The first 'movement' of this response is then followed by a second one, that of God's total forgiveness and so of man's total rehabilitation and reinstatement to fellowhsip with God. Moreover, God's 'change of plan' is not accomplished on a plane apart from God himself, like as when a chess-player merely makes a cynical but surprising new move on the board before him, with the aim merely of humiliating his opponent. The change of plan begins as the Word within God's own heart (see 1 : 3) which has already known what it means to be wounded. Thus God, by his own free choice, necessarily suffers for the sin of man. For God's necessary decision to blot out man, along with those natural processes which man's sin has defiled, means a reversal of the whole plan of creation that had been God's original plan, and about which we have read in detail in chapter 1. Sin, we recall, is an activity, but evil a state.

In the so-called Amarna Letters, which are contemporary with the time of Moses, the verb that is so important to us, and which we are looking at, *n-q-m,* is found used within the vocabulary of the covenant making which lies behind the whole covenant idea that we find in the OT. It spoke of the exercise of imperium on the part of the covenant lord over the lands which are rebelling against his rule. But in J it has come to mean 'executive action' – now with this added extraordinary theological emphasis.

Now, since Gen. 1–11 is in the first place about God before it is about man, from the human point of view we must now ask the question – Has then God failed? Has the insolence of the creature proved stronger than the love of the Creator? The answer is such that we are enabled to see, even in the very next verse, that God is Lord even of evil. Even his expression of loathing at the effect of evil reveals no feeling of glee, no *Schadenfreude*, no whisper of such a phrase as 'I told you so', now that man has spoiled what God had made to be 'very good'. Rather, in a completely positive manner, God's decision is another act of creation, and consequently an act of *re*-creation. For God is able to bring good out of evil, renewal out of judgment, life out of death. Thus creation is not something that has happened once and for all. In the works of Deutero-Isaiah God is spoken of constantly as the Creator, but the word used is not a noun; it is always a participle. God is he who keeps on creating, and he does so by re-creating the new out of the old.

Theologically speaking, however, this passage raises a very important issue about predestination. The 'Single Decree' theologians, ever since the time of Beza, have found this passage too difficult to handle. On the other hand, the Jewish theologian Abraham Heschel notes here what he calls 'the contingency of anger', along with 'the supremacy of compassion' in God's ways with man. We must not, he says, look for a rational coherence in God's actions in history. God's Word is not a dogma, nor an unconditional decree. It would certainly make the mystery of God's ways with man easier to understand if this were so. Once wickedness, for example, had reached its full measure, punishment could then necessarily destroy it. But in the Flood story what is laid down as the basic self-revelation of God, now placed at the head of the Bible, is that beyond justice and anger there lies the mystery of compassion and love.

The problem of evil, as it is discussed in the OT, is pushed back to where it belongs – to God. For example, God is responsible for Satan. 'I form light and create darkness, I make weal' *shalom*, integration, cf. Col. 1 : 17, 'and create woe', *ra'*, evil, disintegration. 'I am the Lord who do all these things', Isa. 45 : 7, RSV. So too with the exercise of God's wrath, so often revealed and described. Isa. 63 : 1–6 speaks of his wading in the blood of his enemies. Hos. 13 : 7 has, 'So I will be to them like a lion, like a leopard I will lurk beside the way . . . I will devour them like a lion, as a wild beast would rend them'. Such passages are incomprehensible to those who today blandly declare that 'God loves you but hates your sins'.

Gen. 1–11 insists that man is a psychosomatic being. Thus man's sins are no less than the actions of the whole man. That is why it is the whole man that must come under condemnation, not just his sins, as if they were merely tacked on to him from the outside. God must therefore plunge the whole man under the Flood. But the Flood story does not end at this point. It declares two more realities. First, the punishment of the Flood has a redemptive purpose. It is not possible to be born again, John 3: 7, unless you first *die*, not your sins, but *you*. So the punishment of the Flood springs from no less than God's unspeakable grace. Second, when God blessed man, Gen. 1: 28, he placed something of himself within man, because that is the meaning of the act of blessing in the OT. This is demonstrated when, to bless another, you made him kneel before you, and laid your hands on his head. So when God sends the Flood upon sinful man, the Flood passes over the head, not only of man, but of God's own presence in man; or, in other words, the Flood story reveals the same reality about God, about evil, and about redemption, as that which we meet with in the NT at the Cross.

God, it seems, bears along with man the consequences of man's sin, and shares, with man, in the costly redemptive process which is his will that all men should know. As the Creator, therefore, God *re*-creates *from within* the evil situation that man has produced by becoming involved in it himself, Ex. 3: 7–8, 12, and so he shares in the pain that the creative process demands. Yet even here God maintains his freedom in his relationship to man by being present in the Flood only in his Word, 1: 3, or in his Spirit, Isa. 63: 11, or in his 'Angel', Ex. 23: 20, – or, could we add, in the NT *in* his Son.

Again, the Flood takes *time* to happen. Both J and P give times and figures for its duration. What they are saying thereby is that God, in the extension of *his* psycho-somatic personality (dare we say?) of which man's person is the image, even as he relates to the world in giving himself room for movement and transition, God moves out of himself in a continuing and developing relationship with man; as Ex. 3: 12 puts it, God speaking to Moses, 'I will become with you . . .'. And in so saying God clearly shows himself to be personal. Thus, as a

Person, God freely enters into the contingencies of history, even into the categories of 'what might not have been'. God is the author of history; that is why its end-purpose is the ultimate renewal of all things. Therefore any kind of *contretemps*, such as diseases, wars, or 'the Flood', are only stages on the journey over which God triumphs *with* man, on the march to the End.

8–10   This new beginning emerges from the prevenient grace of God, who freely decides to alter his plan to make use of just one man in whom his purpose can *rest*; for the name Noah popularly understood, could mean just that. The J passage now concludes with these words. The geneological introduction at v. 9 is obviously from P. It follows from 2: 4a and 5: 1, as we have seen, and leads to the introduction of the names of Noah's three sons. With J the emphasis has been upon God's election of Noah. This has been merely asserted, just as 5: 29 gave us no clue as to why it was Noah who was chosen. God's choice was as truly an act of grace as was the election of Abel at 4: 4. Consequently, following upon this basic story, historically speaking God's elective grace for Moses or for Jeremiah is not explained, for it is not necessary to do so, Ex. 33: 12; Jer. 1: 5. P, on the other hand, gives us more information to reflect upon. Noah, he declares, was a righteous and blameless man: Noah walked with God – the exact phrase used of Enoch at 5: 24. It is evident that the final editor(s) of Genesis were aware of this tension between election and free-will, and to show it they set the two statements down side by side.

Neither of these adjectives suggests that Noah was sinless. Most interpreters have accepted the assumption that here we have the language of the Law of Moses, particularly as it was understood by the Rabbis at the end of the OT period. So they claim these two terms refer to loyalty to the Torah and loyalty to the piety of one who lives in accordance with the 'statutes and ordinances and judgments and commandments' 'which I teach you', 'and do them, that you may live . . .', Deut. 4: 1. Thus the *tsaddiq* (the word rendered by 'righteous' in the RSV) was the man whom God's verdict has justified because he does all this. But if we recall that P's recension and interpretation of J was made in the period of the Exile, we should rather look to see what the root *ṣ-d-q* meant to such a one as Deutero-Isaiah. The latter describes King Cyrus as *tsaddiq*. The context of the word, which occurs at Isa. 41: 26, shows that it could well mean 'victorious' – and this is just how the RSV translates it at Isa. 41: 2. If this is how P understood it, then we are to see that Noah lived a 'victorious' life. Obviously we are meant to connect that idea with what we are also told, that 'Noah walked with God'. The Rabbis, however, insist that *doing* a commandment of God is an act of communion with him. Noah was fully alive to the will of God, and so he *walked* with God. Actually the Talmudic word *Halachah*, meaning that Commentary upon the Law by which a true Jew will *walk* in the sight of god, declares that 'righteous' means being in a right relationship to God within the fellowship of the Covenant. So we can now add that 'blameless' means 'sound, wholesome, a man of integrity'; cf. Job 1: 1; Gen. 17: 1; Ps. 18: 20–24.

At 7: 1 we learn that God had seen how, over a period of years, Noah had been 'righteous' in this sense. He had appropriated the blessing of God, 1: 27, which God had first laid upon him. In the *sight* of God, therefore, he is a man *good for* God's plan. In other words, God's plan can rest in him. In fact, God himself can rest in Noah, despite the total judgment that God has just enunciated upon all flesh, and that would include Noah. For by means of this one human being, even though he is under judgment, God knows that his plan of salvation can still proceed. Thus here we have, parallel with 2: 1–3, God's resting in Noah and God's resting at the end of his creative activity. P in particular, therefore, probes into the theological basis of the Sabbath that is so important to him in his contribution to the remainder of the Pentateuch. Gen. 2: 1–3 is not concerned with the Sabbath institution at all, or with any cult or organization, but only with God's rest. In consequence the Noah story tells us in pictures form what God does with *his* Sabbath rest. What God does with it is to 'evangelize'. This helps us understand the mind of Jesus in his approach to the significance of the Sabbath, and to realize why it especially is a holy day. At Ex. 31: 14 we are told that the Sabbath is holy *for you*. This brings the content of the Noah story down into the very particular history of you and me, as revelation of what we are meant to do with that day in our own case.

The particularism that is a constituent element in God's redemptive activity is made clear again. God needs only one human being to put the whole creative process into reverse. What happens then is that God, for the purpose of man's salvation, reverses what is described in chapter 1, and, (theologically speaking only!), turns the universe back from order into chaos; the watery deep of 1: 2 then recurs. This is what Jeremiah's inner eye perceived, at Jer. 4: 23–26, where the exact words used in 1: 1–3 recur again. Yet Jeremiah hears the Word of the Lord, 4: 27, assuring him, 'Yet I will not make a full end'. So here too, because of Noah, God does not make a full end.

That there was a flood or floods of vast proportions in very ancient times is without doubt. Memories of a great natural disaster have come down to us in the myths and legends of various peoples in Asia, Africa, the Americas, and in Polynesia. The last ice age ended and the ice retreated about 6000 B.C., and as some climatologists believe, it did so comparatively rapidly at least in the northern hemisphere. The quick melting ice would produce the widespread flooding and destruction of life, both human and animal, that the long memories of so many peoples record. There was a lesser cold period about 3500 B.C., sufficient to reinforce the stories of old and which were by then being recorded in writing. Then there was another cold period about 1000 B.C., possibly again sufficient to suggest to J and his generation that surely if Israel's God was indeed Lord of the universe, then there must be *meaning* to the ancient catastrophe which all men knew about. The period 3000 to 1800 B.C. was actually a very wet one over the whole of the Near East. As far east and south as today's Pakistan the Great Sand Desert knew a thriving civilization round what was then Lake Lunkaramsar, near Bikaner. The Sinai desert of Moses' day was nothing like as arid as it is now. Fifty years ago the archaeologist Woolley found evidence that the lower Tigris–Euphrates plain had been flooded about the end of the lesser cold period which we have noted. His spade revealed a thick level of mud that lay both above and below two different civilizations that had flourished in the one city. The geologist confirms the archaeologist Wolley's find with the information that the whole area experienced at that time a period of torrential rains.

Since chapters 6–9 are not a literal description of such a flood, but a pictorial theological interpretation of the meaning of the

judgment of God upon a world that is bent upon its own destruction, only the naïve reader wonders about the size of the
Ark, how all the animals were jammed in, why they did not eat
each other, and since they did not, then how Noah was able to
feed them at all; or such a reader goes climbing up Mount
Ararat to look for any possible remains of the Ark on its summit.

11   So we return to reality, and reality is only to be understood in terms of theology. P repeats what J has said, that God is
heartsick at the *total* corruption he sees, 'the loathsomeness of all
mankind', NEB; for God's total purpose is the redemption of
the total world. So, refusing to let go the last link with man,
God takes Noah into his confidence; in other words a theological affirmation is made within the context of this story which
reveals, first, the pain in the heart of God, second, the total
judgment of God's Word, and third, his determination to bring
about redemption *out of* the pain and the judgment. 'Unless a
seed fall into the ground and die. . . .' The pain arises from
God's necessary decision to destroy his own blessed children,
1 : 28. Evidently God can see no other way to effect the redemption of the world. So the Flood, like that displayed by Woolley,
forms a break in human history. The theological pictures become events in history at such times as, for example, the
Crucifixion and the Holocaust.

God's speech in v. 13 begins with the words *The end of* . . ..
Superficially what follows bears a resemblance to the Babylonian and Assyrian Flood story of Ut-Napishtim, contained
in 439 lines. The transmitters of the story to Israel were possibly
the Hurrians, and in their version, moreover, they use a name
somewhat akin to Noah. But the Babylonian tale is polytheistic,
and tells of the caprice of the gods. The Genesis story, on the
other hand, is *moral*. It deals with ultimate issues of goodness
and truth. It declares that the wages of sin is death, that God
and not the serpent was right when he told Adam that disobedience must inevitably lead to death, 2: 17. Next, it shows
that all life is one, both that of men and that of animals; and
continues to declare that all life is of God, 2: 7, so that life can
be understood only in eschatological terms. Finally, since the
story of the Flood is not recounted as history, but as a speech of
God (shown by inverted commas in modern translations), and
so as the Word of God, then the story, as does the Word, must

stand for ever. Wicked man has no permanent title to life. His life is corrupt, that is, it gives off the odour of death. Corrupt man does not have an immortal soul. Man lives on the edge of the End, a reality, described here, that becomes the theme of all later serious interpreters of God's Word; cf. Amos 8: 2; Hab. 2: 3; Lam. 4: 18; Ezek. 7: 2; 21: 25, 29; Matt. 24. We hear God 'chatting' to Noah how he must *wipe out* man, the horror of the verb showing itself at 2 Kings 21: 13: 'I will wipe Jerusalem as one wipes a dish, wiping it and turning it upside down'. So this means that God's salvation can arise only out of death, and not out of space and time, as is the basic thought of the Hindu Vedas.

So we meet with one of the deep mysteries of the divine mind. Since man, God says to Noah, is 'drinking himself to death', so to speak, God decides to bring about that death in reality. Pharaoh, we read in Exodus, hardened his heart, slowly but surely; but finally it was God who hardened it. If he had not done so, Pharaoh (that is to say, Adam) might have decided to quit the blasphemy of his disobedience, pull himself up by his own bootstraps, and so be able to walk back into the Garden of his own accord, 3: 24. But this divine speech here affirms that man has gone too far ever to be able to do so. 'In God's sight', v. 11, E. A. Speiser translates as 'according to God's (regretful) conclusion'. God must necessarily affirm man's rebellion, Matt. 24: 37–39. 'I will bring a flood of waters upon the earth', he says at 6: 17; in other words, he will undo his creative act, when, in the beginning, 1: 2, the Spirit of God moved over the waters of chaos, Light was born, and the ordered earth sprang into being. So now we glimpse the majesty of God's judgment. That God makes use of a 'righteous and blameless man' does not invalidate the above assertion. God names Noah; Noah finds grace. It is the grace of God which uses Noah the man, not Noah's qualities of mind and heart. The whole story is one of grace. And yet – and herein lies another aspect of the deep mystery of God's being and the paradox of God's grace that are unfolding before us in God's own speech – without Noah it seems that God could do no mighty works, to employ a NT expression, Mark 6: 5. Because of this revelation in this divine speech, therefore, we understand how it was that, *in history*, while *God* brought Israel out of

Egypt, he used the faith of Moses to do so. Noah stands in a right relationship to God, that is to say, he stands before God as a little child, Isa. 57: 15; 66:2; Matt. 5: 3–6. Clearly it is possible therefore for a man, by grace, to remain simple and uncomplicated in a corrupt and violent world.

14–16   The Word now becomes act: 'Make yourself an ark', v. 11. 'Noah did this; he did all that God commanded him', v. 22.

The description that follows fits in with ancient ways of building house-boats on the Nile. 'Make an ark whose frame will be of teak [or cypress, or resinous?], intertwined with basket-work, and smeared all over with bitumen' – a mixture of Egyptian and Mesopotamian features. As one commentator puts it, evidently God can cope even with the oddest specifications! The rooms in the Ark are really 'nests', giving us the idea of cosy warmth in homely cubicles. The word for Ark is an Egyptian loan-word, and is used also for the 'basket' in which baby Moses floated on the waters of the Nile, Ex. 2: 3. It is not the same word as that used for the Ark of the Covenant, Ex. 25: 10, whose shape was much that of a coffin. But the choice of word for Moses' 'basket' explicitly reveals the historicizing of the 'theological ark' described here, even as the frail structure floated on the waters (of chaos?) bearing along helplessly the loving purpose and plan of God *resting* in a baby whom God would use in the next step of his plan.

Noah's Ark was to have three decks, and a lattice window in the form of a skylight rimming it right around the top level, ('roof' in RSV). Its dimensions were to be about 450' by 75' by 45'. We are of course thinking in terms of the age of the giants, 6: 4, so the vessel had necessarily to be of giant proportions. A cubit was 42–45 cm. in length. We are to picture the vessel, not with a sharp bow, but as oblong. We are not given a blue-print here for this huge ship – how could we, in three verses? But more importantly, how could we be given a blue-print for a *theological*, and not a historical ship!

17–22   The word for flood, *mabbul*, in v. 17 occurs here only, but is quoted at Ps. 29: 10. It is descriptive of the chaotic waters of the 'deep' mentioned at 1:2. Thus it means neither the ocean nor a river swollen to become a flood. It is a theological term, used to refer to the mythical picture of the waters above the sky. We recall that in the Babylonian myth the god cut the goddess in two. P takes this myth as his basic picture, and speaks of God dividing the watery chaos in two, but leaving a space between for the creation of the firmament, that is, in between the waters above the firmament, *mabbul*, and the waters underneath. The Second Commandment calls the latter 'the water under the earth', Ex. 20: 4. In other words, God informs Noah that he is about to reverse his original plan and so will turn the ordered universe back into chaos. So, this being theology and not history, we are not to translate the participle by 'I will bring' but by 'I bring', with an all-time connotation to it. Consequently the animals, which have the breath of life in them along with man, although themselves innocent, perish along with culpable man. But Noah and his family have now become the Remnant that God saves.

We note with interest that the covenant which God establishes with Noah at 9: 8 *after* the Flood is gone is promised even before the Flood takes place, v. 18. So it implies a salvation that is not yet mentioned. This is surely nothing less than 'prevenient grace'. But the promise also indicates that, in his elective action, God creates what he elects. So in the later Pentateuch, where we meet with historical situations, we find that Israel's election and creation are inseparable. What is more, so creative is God's election love that he calls, not what is, but what is not, into fellowship with himself. Thus he elects Abraham to be progenitor of a great nation, when physically speaking it is impossible for Abraham to be a father. He makes covenant with a nation that is 'no people' at all, but merely 'a wandering Aramean', Deut. 26: 5.

Now follows the conventional picture of this ever-fascinating story – the animals going in two by two, every species that there is, including even the birds, male and female, in order that no species might perish from the earth. We note, *in history*, how Israel was allowed to take the eggs of any one species for food, but was not allowed to let the species become extinct, Deut. 22: 6. In fact, in general Israel was bidden to care for the whole of the dumb creation, Deut. 25: 4; Prov. 12: 10. Thus it is God's will that man should 'keep them alive', v. 20. Consequently we are to read into v. 21 the suggestion that ideally man should be vegetarian in diet. This notion cannot be pressed, for we are not told what food Noah was to include for the use of the carnivorous beasts he had invited in.

22 'Noah did all that God commanded him.' He did a very strange thing. He built a huge ship on bone-dry ground, miles from any ocean. How his fellow-citizens must have laughed and jeered. When, however, the Word comes to a man *in history* we note again and again, that man may have to act in a mannei that is contrary to nature. It is sufficient to refer only to Gideon, 'whom the spirit of God wore as his clothing', Jud. 6: 34, to note the ludicrous course which that young man chose in order to set his people free.

CHAPTER 7

THE FLOOD

1–10   The divine speech is now taken up by the J tradition, continuing from the section, 6: 5–8. But J narrates it with two changes. First, God asks for one particular group of animals to enter the Ark, but they are not to make their entrance two by two as P had indicated. Instead they are to go seven by seven. And second, this group of animals is to belong to the classification known in the Law of Moses as 'clean'. The use of the number 7, the perfect number, merely emphasizes this belief. The clean animals are meant to be distinct from all other animals, just as Israel, sanctified by God, is distinct from all other nations, Ex. 33: 16. Yet those clean animals which are not taken into the ark do not escape the holocaust any more than the unclean ones. For God is no respecter of persons. On the other hand, the emphasis in this chapter is not on destruction, but upon God's saving love. The method that God uses for the furtherance of this purpose is described here by the use of three times as many words as are needed to express the reality of his wrath. Incidentally, we note that it is through man's obedience to God that the animal kingdom trustfully obeys man, finding peace even between themselves within the confines of the Ark. There is no suggestion here that animals would naturally find peace with man apart from God. Man is meant to be the model for the animal, rather than that man should sink to the level of the animal, 6: 2 (B. Jacob). It has been the great painters rather than the theologians who have understood this reality.

Leviticus 11 lists those animals that are to be regarded as 'unclean'. Deut. 14, alongside those that are unclean, lists those to be considered 'clean'. Evidently P, writing later than J, presumes that the distinction between clean and unclean animals did not apply before God historicized the difference between them through Moses. J, however, continues by agreeing that the unclean animals were to enter in pairs. Unclean animals might not be used for sacrifice. We note that when the Flood subsided Noah 'took of every clean animal and of every clean bird, and offered burnt offerings on the altar', 8: 20. The clean animals were preserved, therefore, not merely for their own sakes, like the unclean animals, but for the greater glory of God. It was for that reason that both they and man were created, cf. Gen. 45: 5.

Finally God warns Noah that there is to be a seven-day pause. It will be a period of awe-ful tension, as Noah waits for the undoing of the seven-day act of creation. How devastatingly this story brings home to us the heinousness of sin. Then, after naming the round figure of forty days and forty nights, a common biblical expression, God's speech is concluded; cf. Ex. 24: 18; 34: 28; Deut. 10; 10; 1 Kings 19; 8; Matt. 4: 2; Acts 1: 3, etc. But at once it is followed by a note to say that Noah was obedient to the Word in every detail, cf. Ex. 39: 42–43. Matt. 24: 38–9 sets his obedience over against a world that was quite uninterested in the fact of God, and which took for granted that a hedonistic life can give full satisfaction. It is not suggested, however, that Noah himself was morally perfect. He is just one member of sinful humanity, 9: 21. What we are told is that Noah *believed God*, just as is said of the historical Abraham – 'Abraham believed God, and it was reckoned to him as righteousness', Rom. 4: 3.

11–16   We note the interwoven narratives, clearly visible in v. 12. In fact 7: 2 actually employs different words for male and female from those found at 6: 19 and 7: 3. Again 7: 6 (following 6: 17), speaks of the *mabbul*, the waters above the sky, crashing down upon the earth. But v. 11 emphasizes rather the waters under the earth, the 'great *tehom*', which now spurts forth from below. Great Tehom, without a definite article, is referred to as if she were indeed the Monster of the Deep of the ancient myths. So we have the waters above, which fall only in the form of rain through the 'windows of heaven', and we have the deeps below working in concert together. This concept of the deep bursting out is reflected in many places, such as Ps. 74: 15; Isa. 48: 21; or the reverse, Job 38: 8–11. It is applied to the historical event of the exodus from Egypt, Isa. 51: 10; Ps. 78: 15. The windows in heaven are mentioned at 2 Kings 7: 2; Isa. 24: 18; Mal. 3: 10, and each time they are opened by God himself.

At this point our narrative makes no mention of a separation between clean and unclean animals. The emphasis rather is that they *all* entered the Ark, *as God had commanded Noah.* This was therefore no chance event in the evolution of nature. It took place by God's command. The various ice ages that, historically, wiped out tens of thousands of varieties of mammals, fish and insects, and enveloped whole races of men, were not mere chance events within the evolution of the various species. These ice ages happened even *as God commanded.* Moreover, the narrative is interested in what *kinds* of animals entered the Ark, just as it tells us what kind of humans did so too. Noah and each of his sons have only one wife apiece. True love cannot exist in harem conditions. True love, as we saw at 4: 19, between one man and one woman, is a basic condition before humanity can hear and obey the Word of God.

As the Remnant figure who escapes the Holocaust, Noah is important. The 'death and resurrection' theme that runs like a thread through the Bible is not just a theological idea. It happens in the lives of men. It happened to Noah at a particular moment in the life he held in trust from God, on February 17th, we might say, v. 11, by our reckoning. Yes, declares P, it was *on that very day.* It is as if *that day* cut time in two – into antediluvian and post-diluvian time. But within the eternal plan of God. 'Feb. 17th' was thus a vital date, not primarily for man, but first of all for God!

Theology is no abstract science. The will and plan of God which theology discusses become incarnate in the lives of men, at particular dates and in particular places. Thus, *historically* speaking, we find this phrase used three times for the institution of the Passover, Ex. 12: 41, so as to emphasize that at a particular time and date God spoke within Israel's life and experience. This view of the divine activity is now well expressed in the words 'and the Lord shut him in . . .'. In faith Noah had gone in. But God then confirmed Noah's faith by an act of his own. This way of speaking comes to us in a manner parallel to that in which we hear that God hardened the heart of Pharaoh. This happened, we read, only after Pharaoh had first chosen to harden his own heart. Life is meant to be lived in earnest, in all integrity; life is clearly not a game.

17–24   By the use of the word *mabbul* we understand

firstly that, not just earth, but the entire cosmos was flooded. Secondly, there is no description of the horror associated with the drowning of millions of men, as we might expect if this narrative were handled by a Hollywood producer. Yet the totality of the Holocaust is vividly expressed by 'all in whose nostrils was the merest breath of life died', v. 22, *Tor*. So the description works backwards from the order of creation as we have it in chapter 1 – man, animals, birds, as if God were rewinding the reel on which the drama of cosmic existence is discernible. This is because the story is not about man, not even about Noah and his faith; it is about God, and about his purposeful, saving act of judgment. This passage thus becomes the basis of the theology (though not in a detailed description) of the Apocalyptic pictures which occur in both Testaments. M. Black, for example, bases the passage Luke 21 : 25 on the theological use of the *mabbul* here. He would translate the word 'sea' by *tohu*, Gen. 1 : 2. (*An Aramaic Approach to the Gospels and Acts*, p. 196.) The same could be said for the meaning of Rev. 21 : 1. Such thinking is unique. To Plato, the universe was 'a living being . . . a perceptible god'; the universe is the sum and substance of all there is. Here, however, God is wholly other than the universe he has created. Again, the Greeks adored Nature for her gifts to man. Biblical man, on the other hand, unlike our modern custom of referring to Mother Earth, regarded Nature rather as man's sister, as we have seen, for she is God's creation as well as is man.

The waters bore up the Ark; the purpose of God is not swallowed by *tohu*; rather, God commands evil to serve the good. Actually, total good comes out of total evil; and so the Ark floats even above the tops of the mountains. God is in complete control of *tohu*, Ps. 24: 1–2; Matt. 14: 25. God could of course totally 'blot out every living thing', and yet continue to control the outcome of his act of judgment. The act of blotting out God leaves to Nature to do, as we learn from the passive of the verb used. So we are reminded that 'unless a grain of wheat falls into the earth and dies, it remains alone; but if it dies, it bears much fruit', John 12: 24. This theology of crisis is to be found in none of the religions of the world. But here, of course, we are not dealing with what is known as religion, which is a term to describe man's search for God. What we meet with here is not religion, but revelation. It is surely extraordinary that J and P have been able, with the help of their final editor, to offer us, in pictorial form, so much profound theology, and to present to us in these eleven chapters the theology of the whole biblical revelation.

No prophet is more aware of the judgment described here than is Amos. Yet he is also sure of God's redemptive purpose to the extent that he can see the back of the coin, the other side of the *end* that has come upon Israel, Amos 8: 2, an *end* which he pictures in terms of Noah's Flood, Amos 9: 5–6. So his book finishes with an expression of just such a faith in the outcome of God's mercy, Amos 9: 14–15. Like Jeremiah, who goes through an agony of mind on this issue, he is fully aware of the tension a believer must experience before he can recognize the relationship between judgment and hope.

'And the waters prevailed upon the earth', v. 24, or 'dominated' it, for 150 days. As we might say, in the plan of God for the total obliteration of his cosmos, we have now reached 11.59 p.m. Nothing is left of creation at all, except a little boat, with 'one household' in it, living in horror and helplessness as they survey the total desolation. There it goes, bobbing on the waters of chaos, helpless, alone, like an interplanetary rocket in the vast spaces of the universe – except for the grace of God, the one thing that ultimately matters. But within that little 'space-ship' there is a foretaste of the world to come, for in it the wolf is lying down with the lamb, and the leopard with the kid, and the calf and the lion and the fatling together, Isa. 11: 6. This then is not just a miracle, a miracle of grace. It is ultimately a promise for the future of God's cosmos, as Isaiah has so clearly stated in his inimitable poem.

CHAPTER 8

GOD REMEMBERS NOAH

1–5   The Bible is not primarily interested in depicting men and women as individuals, nor does it seek to delineate human characters. What is of basic interest to it is what we might describe as 'persons in situations'. This is because it is God who has created those situations. God creates this particular situation now by 'remembering' Noah and *by so doing* he creates the turning-point in the revelation of his purpose. Of course God had not forgotten Noah. That idea is inconceivable. To remember means to bring into the foreground of consciousness. Thus to say that God remembers is merely another way of speaking of his faithfulness, 19: 29; 30: 22; in fact the idea of remembering is a key word in biblical language. On his part man should surely not try to supplement the grace of God, for God is all in all, 2 Cor. 12: 9, by either an act of faith or one of commitment to God. What man must do basically is just to remember in return *what God has done*, Deut. 7: 18; 8: 18; 24: 9; Ps. 77: 11; 119: 55; 2 Cor. 11: 24, and so be glad, thankful and obedient.

Two emphases emerge by the use of this verb to remember. Firstly we glimpse by its use God's true nature, which is one of compassion, concern, loyalty, and love. Secondly, since in the Bible the verb to remember means to recall to the forefront of the mind the object of one's concern, and there to hold it steadily in one's thought, we note how its use comes in parallel with that of the verb to say. When God speaks his Word he performs an action which must inevitably accomplish his will, Isa. 55: 10–11. In the same way, God's act of recalling to the forefront of his mind means here that he is about to make use of Noah in terms of the latter's *name*, 'rest'. This is well illustrated in the words of an Apochryphal Gospel discovered not many years ago. It speaks of Jesus: 'In all the prophets have I [God] awaited thee, that you wouldest come and I might find rest in thee, for thou art my rest', Cf. Gen. 30: 22; Ex. 2: 24; Isa. 63:

11. Then we note also that it is in Noah's darkest hour that God 'remembers' him. But remembering leads to action. Moreover, without the divine action Noah would never have known that he was remembered!

Again a precise date is given for the subsidence of the waters, and for the Ark's resting on the precise spot known as Mount Ararat. This mountain was the highest point known to Israel, being 16,945 feet high. It topped the massif that lay on the edge of the world 'to the east' where Eden lay, 2: 8. From it therefore you looked down on the Caspian Sea, whose waters stretched east to infinity. Thus Ararat was at the opposite end of the world from the Atlas Mountains in Morocco, called after the Greek god whose mighty shoulders held up the sky in the west where the mountain looked out into the infinity of the Atlantic Ocean.

God, then, first remembered Noah; then he blew his wind (or spirit) as he had done in the beginning over the watery chaos, 1: 2. The fountains of the deep obeyed and the waters subsided. And this cosmic activity all took place as a result of God's determination to *rest* his purpose of redemption in one human family. Incidentally it is interesting to recall that the World Council of Churches has chosen as its emblem a little ship, floating on the waters of chaos, but in which God has chosen to rest his purpose of saving love for all men.

6–12 J now takes up the theme. Things continue to work in reverse: 'At the end of forty days' (cf. 7: 4, 17) Noah sends off a raven. This was a custom in the navigation of ancient days. But the raven, the bird of prey, the harbinger of death, did not return. But even that negative message was in reality a promise, in that Israel saw the raven as the instrument of God, 1 Kings 17: 4 ff. For the raven was a scavenger; he cleaned up the earth of what would else become putrid corpses. Just like Satan, in Job 1: 7, another instrument of God, he goes to and fro over God's creation in the service of God. Noah next tries a dove. But she tells him nothing either – at first. For at first she finds no *ma-noah*, no place to rest her foot. The family have thus to face the bitter disappointment that God does not answer man's prayers on demand, nor does he allow man to discover that 'all things work together for good' in a mechanical manner. The family has to wait, wait for the symbol of the Spirit, to fulfil their hopes. So here we have the pictorializing of the slow ways of God with man, of which the Prophets were deeply aware.

These verses are full of poetry and art. They offer us the very feel of the atmosphere of waiting in hope – 'Watchman, what of the night?', Isa. 21: 11; also Luke 2: 25; Mark 15: 43; Acts 1: 4; Rom. 8: 19, 23–25. Is the promise of 5: 29 to become true or not? And what of the covenant promised at 6: 18? Yet has not God spoken, so that his Word must come to pass – or will it? In the end the dove does come back *to him*, in entire trust in a man. We watch Noah gently cupping the tired little bird in his hands, and see the dove nestling back amongst her friends of the animal creation. So we are enabled ourselves to identify with the hopes and aspirations of the whole family within the Ark as they wait and wait once again for another long seven days. And now we know that it is not man's faith that ultimately matters, it is God's faithfulness alone; for without the latter our faith would be vain.

And then it happened. The dumb little bird did not know that it was a harbinger of peace, nor that it was the instrument of a human scientific experiment. Yet it heralded the dawn of the new world, clean and fresh, a new creation. Indeed it is that 'joy cometh in the morning'. 'An olive twig!', they cry. The sign, the symbol of the promise of God, a promise that continues throughout the whole Bible. For we meet throughout it with the fact that God has made covenant after covenant both with Israel and with individuals within Israel, and then finally gave his promise of the new covenant, Jer. 31: 31, that heralds the ultimate words: 'Behold I make all things new', Rev. 21: 5. Yet all that Noah had in his hand was a tiny two-inch twig of a tree whose stem was still below the waters of chaos. Yet that was sufficient to let Noah *know* that 'the waters had subsided from the earth'. The earth was not yet dry, the new world had not yet been born. But now Noah was able to say 'I know', and not just 'I believe'; 'I know' that God, in the new aeon, will give back to man his true domain, the earth, the very soil from which he had first formed man's body. So now, as von Rad puts it splendidly, 'The world judgment of the Flood hangs like an iron curtain between this world age and that of the first splendour of creation'. Thus, in, through, and beyond the judgment there must indeed lie both resurrection and life.

13–19   The new era begins, as our author expresses it in his own peculiar theological reckoning, in the year 601, on the first day of the first month. This post-diluvian era is the new era of grace. By employing the number 601 P declares that the seventh century has begun. This chosen number of his thus maintains a parallel with the dawn of the seventh day of creation, 2: 2. The newly created earth could now experience for itself that Rest in which God dwells eternally. On that new day the earth was 'leached out', v. 14. This is not the ordinary word for 'dry up' that occurs at v. 13. Since even the highest point on earth had been under 25 feet of water, every inch of soil on the earth must have been fully 'fumigated' from the pollution it had suffered at the hands of man, 3: 17; 4: 11. God had thus now redeemed the *earth* – at the cost of both pain and suffering and finally death.

Then God said to Noah: 'Go forth', out of the safety of the Ark, where you have a roof over your head. Go out and face the unknown possibilities of the fresh new world. You and your family are free, the animals are free, as are the birds *and the snakes*, free to multiply and fill the earth. So the original blessing, expressed at 1: 22, is here renewed, for we are now in a new situation. The past is over and done with, *all* go forth from the Ark, by families, in the fellowship that God has planned for the new era.

20–22   Noah displays the response that God expects ('the Lord smelled the sweet odour') as a result of his prevenient act of grace in blessing man; Noah displays gratitude. He is thankful for grace, and thankful for God's salvation. If it had not been for the grace of God he and his family would have perished in the holocaust. In other words, as we see here, we who are the descendants of Noah do not have to make a first discovery of the world of faith; we only have to recover it. Faith is not a *terra incognita*, an unknown land; it is rather a forgotten land (J. Neusner, *Understanding Jewish Theology*, 1973, p. 28). So our quest for God is really to return to God. Our thinking of him is really a recall, a remembering of what he has done. The Hebrew word for repentance, *teshubhah*, means just that, viz. 'return'. Yet it also means 'answer'. For returning to God is also an answer to what he has said in his Word. Our gratitude is to be expressed in terms of sacrifice. No theology of sacrifice is expounded here. But we see that man's first *work* on earth is to build an altar. And this altar is to be for a purpose of love. Noah sacrifices not only on his own behalf, but also on behalf of his family, and even on behalf of the animal creation. Consequently since you must employ pain and death if you are to have a sacrifice, even in this fresh, clean new world, the basic significance of the existence of pain is made manifest. Moreover, the sacrifice is to be made only by the use of a clean bird or a clean animal. This principle expressed here is never abandoned, even in the NT, cf. Luke 2: 24. Since we live in a period when only too frequently historical positivism and hermeneutical interest go their separate ways, I would dare to suggest that we try to close the gap between them by recognizing that a straight line runs directly from this verse to the meaning of the death of Christ.

Noah's sacrifice is first of all a sacramental act. By means of it, in symbolic form God actually deals with man. First it is God who ordains the action, not man, and God even provides the beast for the sacrifice. The latter's death thus becomes an expiation for fallen mankind. For deep in man's heart he knows that only God can expiate human sin and then only of his grace. Second, Noah's sacrifice is to be understood in the light of the apotropaic sacrifices of the ancient world. Noah is acting out a petition to God to turn away his wrath. God did indeed do so. He smelled the pleasing odour and said *to* his heart, within himself, 'I will never again curse the ground . . .'. And of course we in our turn recognize that this 'typical' promise of God is absolute in reality. God in his grace lets himself be deeply moved in his heart by the act of man which he himself had initiated. Thus the whole action is virtually of God alone. Man does not eat of the meat of this sacrifice at all. All that man can do is express thanks, and show by his acts that he recognizes that the one who is saved is bound up totally with him who is his Saviour. And so what we read about at 8: 21 becomes the reverse of what we learned at 6: 6–7; cf. Hos. 11: 8–9; Isa. 54: 9–10. God cannot again curse the ground because of man's rebelliousness. In fact the total reverse is the final truth about the nature of God. In response to the sacrifice God says, '*Ki* I will never . . .'. This little particle introduces an oath or a strong declaration. What is meant is, 'I swear that . . .', an absolute statement such as we find again at 9: 15.

The last verse therefore speaks of what is one of the great themes of the OT. It describes in agricultural and meteorological language the *ḥesed* of God. This is the word used to describe the content of God's Covenant, which had been promised at 6: 18 and which is the subject of the next chapter. It is the steadfast, dependable, loyal, unshakeable love of God that marks it off from all man's ideas about the meaning of love. Man's ideas about love can be mixed up with sex, with natural family affection, with friendship, with sentiment, with transient expressions of tenderness. Hosea applies this general expression of *ḥesed* made here to God's unalterable loyalty to Israel, that dissolute wife whom God himself has elected. Perhaps such love may best be described in the simple words of the hymn, quoted before, 'O love that wilt not let me go'. This *reliable* love of God will be witnessed to in the *reliable* succession of the seasons.

Finally man discovers that the love of God is such as this verse describes only because both God and man together have now gone through the waters of judgment, *out of* which, and not *after* which God has re-created, firstly, the heavens and the earth, and secondly, Man, by means of his forgiveness and grace. Clearly God's creativity never ceases.

CHAPTER 9

GOD THE COVENANTER

1-7   God does not change; only his plan changes. The blessing referred to here is that which God has already given at 1 : 28 (both this passage and Gen. 1 are from the hand of P). But now there is no mention of creation being 'very good'. In fact, from now on we meet with neither an optimistic view of nature and of man, nor a pessimistic one. We meet with a realistic view. Part of that realism is that man can know true freedom only under Law. Law is the condition of the new beginning, or, as Tillich put it: 'Law is the form loves takes when we are estranged from it'. At 4: 11 it was man who was the legal guardian and avenger of the sanctity of human life. Now it is God who is. The unlimited violence that natural man supposed was his right, 4: 24; 6: 11, is now regulated in terms of the law of an eye for an eye.

Even the animals are now under law. That fact does not give man unlicensed power over them, however, even though God authorizes him to control such things as plagues of locusts, mosquitoes, rabbits, or germs, Deut. 11 : 25. Man is to rule over the animals – under God. So his power over the animals is to be a merciful power. We think of the conscience of man today, e.g. in the matter of preserving baby seals in the Arctic and whales in the southern ocean. In other words, man's control of Nature is to be bound up with the moral law, Ezek. 33: 25.

But this passage goes behind the Law of Moses, in line with the fact that Jesus consistently appealed to Genesis over against the Law. '*Every* moving thing that lives shall be food for you.' And great emphasis is laid upon the sacredness of *life*, to the extent that modern man is challenged to examine such issues as suicide, abortion, and euthanasia in the light of this biblical revelation. Basically we are not dealing here with a ritual law, but with a moral command. The state of life, *hayyim*, is holy. Therefore it is unthinkable that one should eat part of an animal that is still alive, the symbol of its life being the blood itself. This is expressed apodictically, in the words 'You must not . . .'. Since God is the owner of all life, including that of the animals, each man and woman, and each animal and bird is a unique creation, and man is still made in the image of God.

Three times over we read the phrase, spoken of God, '*I* will require . . .'. A judicial sentence of capital punishment can therefore come only from God, *elohim*. This word, we note, is used to describe those judges who must necessarily pass the judgment of death; they do it as from God, Ex. 21 : 6; 22 : 8.

Verses 6 and 7 form a high point in revelation. Their contents are to be remembered for all time, and to that end they are expressed in poetry:

> Whoever sheds the blood of man,
>> By man shall his blood be shed.
> For in the image of God,
>> Made he humanity.
> But you, be fruitful and multiply,
>> Swarm on the earth and multiply in it.

Jesus, at Matt. 26 : 52, regards this passage to be as truly the revealed mind of God as is the Decalogue.

In later centuries the Rabbis codified this passage and enlarged upon it. They produced what became known as the *Noahic Code*, and declared it to be the basic minimal standard of morals that God has laid upon the Gentile nations, for they are not expected to conform to the Law of Moses. This Code is the Code of Natural Religion, and as such seems to have been known in essence even to Amos, as we can see in Amos chapters 1–2. Acts 15 : 20 also seems to refer to this Noahic Code. The Code took various forms, but the *Jewish Encyclopedia*, 1904, II, 648–50, gives the following as the standard form it took in Rabbinical times:

(1) The establishment of courts of justice.
(2) The prohibition of blasphemy.
(3) The prohibition of idolatry.
(4) The prohibition of incest.
(5) The prohibition of murder.
(6) The prohibition of robbery.
(7) The prohibition of eating flesh cut from a living animal.

This passage has been of immense importance in the thought of man.

8–17 God's next act is to bless the humanity that is meant to live the moral life on the basis of the above Code, with its emphasis upon the value of life. Finally he does a very strange and unique thing that no other god, ancient or modern, has ever sought to do; he 'erects his covenant' (in the sense of its being a 'sign-post') with the humanity of the new age. So the word of blessing is here expanded into the area of grace. The whole passage is repetitious. The final editor has used both of his sources without too much streamlining, for he wants to emphasize the importance of the Covenant. For it is God who made it, not man.

As we have said, God does not change, Mal. 3: 6. But the revelation of his grace grows unendingly. And here again we have revelation so expressed that it is to be seen as the very Word of God, v. 8; for the first word of the divine speech is *I*. Moreover, what we meet with is more than self-revelation; it is divine commitment, commitment not just to men, but even to the beasts of the field. In other words, God here *undertakes* for them. Both man and beast had been safe before in the Ark. Now they are to continue to be safe in the new era of grace that has dawned. B. Jacob calls this 'God's great-hearted universalism'; cf. Matt. 5: 45. For there is no suggestion here that nature is in some sense inferior to man. The Hebrew word *ra‘*, evil, is used by the great prophets alike of earthquakes, nature red in tooth and claw, cancer, and human lust and greed. In our day we can now analyze how man's *ra‘* has brought about ecological disasters and the pollution of the earth and sea. Creation is one, and God commits himself to all of it without distinction. The Covenant is made with all parts of the one single socio-natural community that is to be found on the planet Earth.

'Behold, I establish my covenant', 'between my Word and the earth,' adds the Targum. This word 'covenant' has very ancient roots. Originally *berith* did not mean an agreement between two equal parties, as it might on occasions mean in history. Rather, it was an *imposed* situation, describing a liability or obligation felt by the giver of the covenant. Ps. 111: 9 reads: 'He has commanded his covenant for ever'. This is in agree-

ment with the early historian at Jud. 2: 20. That is to say, the
Covenant that God commands is an absolute; it is unconditional; it is unilateral. That it is an imposed covenant that is
spoken of here is shown clearly in that animals cannot respond
any more than can babies when they are circumcised. 'He
loved us before we loved him' is a phrase that could not have
been written without the reality expressed here in Gen. 9. Man
cannot make an agreement with grace; he can only accept
grace in awe and gratitude.

Gen. 9 does not speak of the historical covenants that God
made with Abraham and the Patriarchs, nor of that which he
made with Israel, Ex. 19: 1–6. Far less does it speak of any new
covenant that he would one day make with the House of Israel,
Jer. 31: 31. What it does do is to speak of the very nature of
God, whose revealed relationship with his creation is to be
known in terms of his total commitment to it. We talk only too
glibly today of our need to make a commitment to God. The
reality, however, the good news revealed to us here, is that
God has already committed himself to us! Moreover, since such
is God's nature, that he is *there*, not for his own sake, but for the
sake of 'all flesh', even of a sparrow that falls to the ground, then
we are not surprised that he chooses to relate to man in an
ever-new covenant commitment that never ceases to reveal
the self-emptying of his nature; cf. Rom. 11: 1–2. Other
passages speak of God's 'cutting' a covenant (evidently part of
the ritual of sacrifice accompanying the act), e.g. in Deut. But
the LXX prefers to translate 'cut' by a verb such as 'give' or
'donate' in those passages that deal with the historical covenants. It evidently chose its terms in the light of Gen. 9, just as
elsewhere the Hebrew uses 'give', or 'establish', 'institute', or
'set up'. This last verb suggests the idea that we can see the
covenant standing erect, visible like an eternal monument.
Clearly this early passage in the Bible is saying what later books
declare categorically, viz. that God is love.

God here reveals his own freely chosen obligation to man, in
the light of which he makes an absolute promise that the era of
grace cannot revert to the era of chaos; or, to put it in modern
language, God makes it plain that he is going to win. God
assures us that it is not Mystery that controls all reality, in the
form of an irrational, inscrutable and blind power, the Maat of

the Egyptians, Moira among the Greeks, or Pta in Indian thought. Rather he warns that we are not to settle peacefully in the bland belief that since God is in heaven, all is therefore well with the world. God's covenant is the astonishing assurance that God is actually in need of man. As A. J. Heschel declares, in *God in Search of Man*, 1955, p. 68, 'The ultimate is not a law but a judge, not a power but a father'.

This memorable truth is expressed again in the phrase 'the sign of the covenant', v. 12:

> This is the sign of the covenant
>   which I am bestowing
>   between me and you;
> And between all living creatures
>   that are with you for all ages to come.
> My bow I have set in the clouds;
>   it will become the covenantal sign
>   between me and the earth.

The words of the oath accompanying the 'sign' are repeated at vv. 13, 15, 16, and 17, four times in all, as if, still speaking poetically, the bow were visible from north, south, east, and west. Again, the sign in all its beauty emerges from the darkness caused by the thundercloud. God, it seems, does not abolish the darkness. God creates the thundercloud. In fact his light can appear to man only because darkness is a fact.

13   In the ancient mythologies the warrior god made himself manifest with his bow and arrow, ready to destroy his enemies. And so the rainbow was often the sign of the wrath of the gods, especially since the phenomenon appeared in conjunction with thunder and lightning. Here, at the Flood, God's wrath has indeed broken over his creation in an unprecedented rainstorm. For God is the warrior God, Ex. 15: Isa. 63: 1–6, who is 'trampling out the vintage where the grapes of wrath are stored'. After the Flood, therefore, by every reckoning, there should have appeared the Bow of Wrath, hanging over the world of men like the sword of Damocles; cf. Ps. 7: 12–13; 18: 14; Hab. 3: 9–11. But what we meet here invites intense surprise. The Bow of God, we are told, is there to protect and care for God's creation, not to destroy it. The Bow is the 'sign' not of wrath but of mercy, the sign of the *everlasting* covenant that God has now made 'with all flesh that is upon the earth'.

The rainbow has in fact become the guarantee of God's patience *that will never end*, in that the rainbow will continue to reappear so long as the earth remains; and each time it will reassure man that even 'the gates of hell' will not prevail over the grace of God's personal self-commitment to the restitution of his creation. A flood may last a mere 150 days, but the rainbow reappears unendingly.

'I will remember', says God, using the fascinating verb we examined at 8: 1, 'my covenant between me and you.' And so today the living God thinks on *me* in my rebellious state of mind in such a way that his will for my salvation and peace answers my will for my own self-destruction and reversion to chaos. I did not ask God to make a covenant with me. I did not respond to him by committing myself to him in return. If I had tried to do so, I would have been insulting the unspeakable grace of God. And so the story ends, not in strife, but in peace, the very peace of the God of peace.

Yet the implication of this ending cannot be ignored. Though the Covenant is to last for ever, that foreverness includes the period of punishment for breaking the covenant which is bound up with the nature of the God who established the covenant in the first place. For this reason the Great Prophets can suggest the possibility of the *complete destruction* of Israel as the natural outcome of the covenant. Yet, in so doing, they had to wrestle with the mystery that the love of God is the 'O love that wilt not let me go' kind, which goes beyond all human assumptions about the divine. We should note that the casual reader may mislead himself about the significance of the rainbow. He may suppose that when man sees this sign in the sky it reminds him of the mercy of God. But that is not what we read. What we find is that when *God* sees the rainbow he reminds *himself* of the true nature of his own being! So the prophets had to envisage that which is logically, theologically, and morally impossible, viz. that the God who is bound to Israel in covenant just as a husband is bound to his wife might have to suffer *with* Israel that very damnation which his own act of commitment in covenant had revealed. This is what Ezekiel made clear through his traumatic experience of finding that the death of his wife, the 'delight of his eyes', Ezek. 24: 15, was a revelation through human experience of God's experience at the 'death' of his beloved Bride, Zion, Ezek. 33: 21. For it was only once Jerusalem had fallen that Ezekiel could hear the promise, 'I will make with them a comprehensive, total covenant'.

How very important this passage is for a grasp of the whole biblical revelation. It states absolutely that God is the God of covenant, that he is the great Covenanter, that God's relationship to his creation is in terms of the covenant that *he himself* has erected. The Covenant makes the astonishing affirmation that God is in need of man. This passage does not of course describe a historical incident when God acted to create this relationship; rather it offers us a theological picture about what God is like; consequently the rest of the Bible, both Old and New Testaments, depends for its interpretation very much on this passage. Since there is only one God, there can be only one covenant. This covenant cannot be quite simply annulled at any time. Isa. 54: 10 would be well translated by 'My comprehensive covenant shall not be removed', in line with the verse from Ezekiel above, for such terms as these bring out the basic meaning of the Hebrew noun *shalom*. Because of this 'total' meaning of the word, the truth that Deutero-Isaiah witnesses to continually falls into place. It is that God, because of the Covenant, keeps on continually creating and so re-creating. In the midst of the 'chaos' of the life that Israel had to lead in exile in Babylon God was still creating a new situation. Isa. 51: 9–11 declares that, just as God had once made a path for the redeemed to cross over the Sea of Reeds of old (a historicizing of the absolute revelation made in Gen. 1: 1–3), so he was now about to do the same again, not by offering a different covenant, but by being faithful to his one and only covenant of redeeming love.

Paul is therefore right to speak of the covenant made through Moses with Israel as merely *palaios*, meaning 'ancient', and *not* 'old' or 'out-of-date'. And he is right to quote Jer. 31: 31, 'I will make a new covenant with Israel', and in using the Greek word *kainos*. For if Paul had misunderstood Gen. 9: 9, then he would have called the *new* covenant in Christ *neos*, meaning 'completely different'. But *kainos* refers to the one and only covenantal relationship that can exist, although its form has been remodelled in terms of the words: 'I will put my law within them, and write it upon their hearts; and I will be their God and they will be my people', Jer. 31: 31.

We note that this is to be a new covenant, and that it is to be made with *Israel*, even as the ancient covenant made at Sinai, Ex. 19, was made with Israel. Thus it is not to be a different covenant, far less is it to be made with a 'new Israel'. Such an inference would be both antisemitic and Marcionite (Marcion sought to rid the early Church of the OT on antisemitic grounds), and it would deny the continuity of the Israel of God, the People of God, comprising both the Jews and the Church, from Abraham to our day. The New Covenant in Christ thus completes the Sinai Covenant, yet only because (1) it makes an event in history of the Covenant spoken of in Gen. 9, that is, it is meant *for all men*; and (2) it reveals finally the *ḥesedh* of God (see the end of the previous chapter), that is, God's complete faithfulness and loyalty to the human race. Thus because of the uniqueness of the only Covenant, and because of God's loyalty, those who make covenant theology their starting-point rest securely as to the past, so that they can remain open to the future in terms of the Reformation principle, *semper reformanda* (always to be reformed) in all things to do with the application of the biblical faith to the ever-new and ever-changing world that has followed the Flood.

18–19   Our editor now selects from very early sources of tradition. While v. 18 reiterates 6: 10 in declaring that the fresh new world was repopulated through Shem, Ham, and Japheth, emphasis is now placed upon Ham. The Covenant is made, of course, with all nations. Yet we are left with the mystery that God has actually bound himself in a loving relationship with Canaan, and not just with Shem. (We note that though Ham may mean the Egyptians and other dark-skinned peoples, Canaan, for theological reasons, is singled out of Ham's sons.) Israel, as the Covenant People of God, considered themselves descended from Shem. But Israel's neighbours, the Canaanites, were another matter. Much of the 'Law of Moses', as it grew and developed over the centuries, was formulated in direct opposition to the ways of Canaan. The Canaanites were polytheists. They had created their gods (and goddesses) after their own image; whereas Israel believed that Yahweh had created man after *his* image! 1: 26. The gods were sensual, vicious, ready to take offence, mean and selfish. More-over, they were the apotheosis of man's natural instincts, so that they were worshipped *because* of their sexual prowess and strength of arm. These two qualities, so-called, are summed up in the nature of the god Baal. In biblical times he was worshipped under the form of a bull. For the bull enshrines the physical strength and the sexual domination by the male over the female that the Canaanite considered to be the true marks of male *machismo* and therefore most worshipful by man. We meet here then with a vastly different ethos from that summed up in the words: 'Noah was a righteous man, blameless in his generation; Noah walked with God', 6: 9. By the use of the name Ham, therefore, our author actually places under the care of Yahweh all those heathen nations known to Israel who followed abominable practices.

The name Japheth makes another emphasis. It signifies the sea-peoples, the Philistines, the Cretans, the Phoenicians, and eventually even the Greeks. Some of these nations were ingenious in building a commercial empire, in expansion of trade, and in the development of intellectual pursuits. They were not however necessarily vicious like the Canaanites. All of them, however, were religious. But here again all that they did possess was 'religion', that is to say, human ideas about the divine. 'Shem', on the other hand, possessed revelation; Shem had experienced the living God himself. Yet all three names are placed together in the one sentence. All three are therefore regarded as being on an equality before God, whose covenant includes them all. It was from these three, then, that 'the whole earth was peopled'.

20–28   In the new world we find repeated what we have already met at 4: 2: 'Noah began straight away to be a farmer'. So the *adam-adamah* theme of chapter 2 is still apparent. While Noah is still Adam, he is Adam forgiven, he is Adam granted a new start in a clean new world. And what a new start this might indeed have been. 'Out of the ground which the Lord has cursed this one shall bring us relief from our work and the toil of our hands', 5: 29. Are we then now in a new Garden of Eden? Throughout Israel's long story in the rest of the OT the ideal that is expressed here was at least looked for. For Noah planted a vineyard; cf. 1 Kings 4: 25; 2 Kings 18: 31; Isa. 36: 16; Micah 4: 4; Zech. 3: 10.

Noah, however, is still an immature child in this new-born

world. He has yet much to learn from experience and especially that one cannot live one's life on earth unscathed. He has to discover that the earth can still bring forth grapes that may lead to the knowledge of good and evil, 2: 17. Life is an adventure. The possibility of evil is infused in all elements of living. Medical scientists inform us that we are born with arsenic in our bones. Thus drinking the fruit of the vine is an aspect of discovering whether wine really gladdens the heart of man, Ps. 104: 15, or turns him into an animal. That is why the phrase in the Lord's Prayer is so relevant at all times, 'lead us not into temptation'.

Man nobly and heroically seeks to reach the South Pole, but perishes in the attempt. A scientist discovers the mysterious beneficial effects of X-rays, but perishes himself from their harmful influence. In Jacob's blessing of his sons he prophesies that Judah must find out for himself what reality is, Gen. 49: 10–12. For all life is a calculated risk whose challenge must be taken up if the good life is ever to result for the good of all. Thus the new wine is a symbol of the open possibilities of the new age, Num. 13: 23; Joel 3: 18. Under no circumstances are we to bring a moral judgment to bear upon Noah as he falls drunken in his tent. Man learns only from experience. In our day, every material discovery brings its compensatory disadvantages, road deaths from the development of the internal combusion engine, unspeakable devastation from the discovery of nuclear fission. Noah is the 'guinea-pig', so to speak, from whom all mankind has been able to learn that along with drunkenness goes moral laxity, and that the drugging of the higher powers of human consciousness leads to sexual licence.

Here enters the significance of Ham to the story. Ham, that is to say, Israel's Canaanite neighbours, supposes that a sexual failing is an occasion for mirth and for the telling of dirty stories. Noah's action, following upon his drunkenness, however, is merely the symbol of the new fertility required by God's blessing being repeated from 1: 26. The incident may merely mean that Noah and his wife were naked together in their tent even as were Adam and Eve when God introduced them to each other. Shem and Japheth, on the other hand, in pity upon their father whom they love, and who, they see, has fallen into danger by taking a pioneering risk on their behalf, with true filial piety cover over his nakedness. (We are to remember that the word 'nakedness' can at times also mean 'a man's wife'.) In other words, we have in these verses a profound revelation of the difference open to man between taking up the challenges of life seriously and reverently, and in supporting one another in loyalty and mutual forgiveness when things go wrong and when a pioneering activity ends in disaster – and between the flippant approach to the dignity and courage of the human spirit that is the mark of the Canaanite religion in every age. A sample of such thinking is apparent in the 'Playboy' literature of our day. But also from another angle the pietist too is often unwilling to 'take the risk' of faith. The Rechabites of the OT as a group were marked for their zeal for the Lord. This they showed by refusing to let wine cross their lips, Jer. 35: 5-19. Yet these estimable people were soon left behind in the on-going sweep of history, and they have made scarcely a mark upon the story of Israel.

Noah's curse is clearly meant to appear as the revelation of essential truth. So, being prophetic interpretation of history, it is expressed memorably in poetry. He who is a slave to his appetites is a slave indeed. The phrase before us means actually 'the lowest of slaves'! But 'blessed by the lord my God' be those who commit themselves to God's revelation as Shem has done. So Noah's words are not 'I bless you'; instead they are the assurance heard in prophetic utterance that *God* will do all the blessing upon those who seek to take life seriously and work co-operatively with him.

It is to this end, therefore, that our editor handles the trinity of names as he does, each with a theological slant. By the way, Canaan is not the youngest son of the three; he is Noah's grandson. B. Jacob gets round the discrepancy in this verse by translating 'youngest' as 'immature'. However, our editor is not concerned with such literal niceties. Rather he is very much concerned to emphasize the degradation of the Canaanite way of life, so that he readily slips from the name Ham to that of Canaan to make his point crystal clear. Actually, by the end of the OT era a popular name for a Gentile living in Palestine as a descendant of Canaan was 'a man without a father'. Shem, on the other hand, later identified with Israel and later still with the Jewish people of Jesus' day, had in fact by NT times preserved and built up, by contrast with the Gentile peoples, a beautiful family life. Israel had learned that the family alone is the seed-bed for holy living. The curse upon Canaan is therefore not so much creative of Canaan's dissolution as a people – for it was not God who did the cursing, but Noah – rather it was the revelation of the *fact* of that very dissolution.

At the same time the blessing upon Shem is a revelation of the *fact* that those who accept the challenges of life discover that they have God with them. The name Shem means Name. God dwells in the form of his Name YHWH in Shem's midst, Ex. 6: 3; 33: 19. So God himself enters into all possible crises such as that the juice of the grape *may* intoxicate, that the natural sexual urge in man *may* turn him into a Canaanite and lead him to cultic prostitution and the consequent disintegration of the human personality, Lev. 18: 24. But it is from the *risk* of drunkenness that Noah, by God's blessing, can become a real man and live on, walking with God, for another 'three hundred and fifty years'. This length of days might have been Canaan's heritage too, for the Canaanites too were Semites, *Shem*ites. But they had disclaimed the Covenant of God.

Again, it is from facing the realities of life with simplicity and sincerity that Japheth too can grow and enlarge. God 'japheths' Japheth, that is to say, he 'makes his dominion wide' in the world. Still more, this has become a *fact* of history now that God has blessed man's dominion, 9: 7. But we should note that the name Japheth can also mean 'beauty'. Thus the name may also refer to the cultural gifts known to such nations as the Greeks. In the end, however, the Gentiles will surely bring their riches and their wisdom and lay these at the feet of Israel's God, Isa. 60.

It is in the tents of Shem, however, that God dwells in particular. I believe that this is how we are to read v. 27b. For God did, it was believed, dwell, or *rest* (cf. *'noah'*), 2 Chron. 6: 41, in the midst of the tents of Israel, first in the Tabernacle, Ex. 40: 35, then in the Temple, 1 Kings 8: 29, and then finally in his Word made flesh, John 1: 14. Targ.Onk. preaches here, however, by translating 'the Shechinah will dwell in the tents of Shem'. This word was a technical term for the indwelling Presence of God. Yet, obviously, it influenced the choice of term that we find in the Prologue to the Fourth Gospel, John 1: 14. We note that Shem is not praised. Shem is no 'better' than

Japheth. It is Shem's *God* who is praised. Shem is merely the elect of God, who, in his wisdom, has elected to dwell in the tents of Shem. This reality summons Israel to remember that she is not Canaan and she is not Japheth, by God's choice, though these peoples share the Holy Land with her. This is therefore a picture of what the world is like at all times.

And Noah died. His limited span of life on earth on both sides of the divide has eschatological significance in itself. Naturally, because God had rested in him. All that God had done, through and for him was now complete. God's completed action was therefore valid and would stand not only in time throughout Noah's life but also throughout eternity as well. For this reason our editor has undertaken to record the fascinating story of Noah so as to show that it is theologically significant and ultimately *important* for all generations to come.

Chapter 10

THE TABLE OF NATIONS

With this Table of the Nations we have moved from pictorial theology as such, as we have called it, to a new type of writing. This chapter contains a serious attempt to write history, in the same sense as the so-called Succession Narrative in 2 Sam. 9–20; 1 Kings 1: 1–2: 12 is history writing. The Table of the Nations is set down with an attempt at scientific objectivity; but there is also an added factor. One feels, rather than reads, that the lists of names have been compiled *sub specie aeternitatis*, so that a divine plan unfolds for us as we read the mere lists of names, that plan whose *meaning* has been unveiled in chapters 1–9, and whose outcome will become clear in the succeeding chapters.

Chapter 10 is a combination of the deeply theological writing of P, whose material appears as one intact section in it, and of fragments of J. P's material follows from 5: 32, being reintroduced by the wording of 10: 1, 'These are the generations . . .'. Yet chapters 5 and 10 are dissimilar. 5: 1–5 connects back to the creation and the birth of man, and then speaks of the work of grace throughout the whole development of man's civilization. Most of the chapter almost monotonously speaks of God's gracious plan for man in giving him birth, then caring for him over a planned period of life, his reproduction, and then his death. Chapter 10, however, looks forward and not backwards; The impulse to this, however, is still the blessing of God, 'Be fruitful and multiply and fill the earth'.

The Table also declares categorically that all mankind is one, since all derive from Noah's three sons. Yet even behind that fact lies the oneness of God. Thus the Table is not interested in the ethnic divisions of mankind, nor does it ever make reference to the colour of the human skin. The fair Greeks here hold no separate place from the black Sudanese. The list is political, however, and it takes for granted that God has created all men of all colours to be political animals. God gave each nation a

territory for itself. Again, since the purpose of the list is not
'religious', we are not meant to find a theological meaning in
every name. Instead we are to look for *relationships* between
nations, as they become linked in cultural, linguistic, historical,
and national groups. This list is important. P does not write
about 'mankind', a word beloved by the present-day anthro-
pologist; nor does he use the word 'society', a term beloved by
the humanist sociologist. P's interest is in *peoples*, persons
grouped politically and culturally, people who live in defined
geographical areas.

Roughly speaking, the *Shem* nations are those living east and
north of Israel (including Israel herself), especially those closely
related to her, such as Edom, Moab, and Ammon. The *Ham*
nations are those under the rule of Egypt, stretching to the
then known areas of the Upper Nile, while J adds in the peoples
of Mesopotamia. Canaan is included also in this classification.
The *Japheth* nations dwell largely on the north shore of the
Mediterranean and in Asia Minor.

This is essentially a highly trustworthy document rooted in
the cultural awareness of the ancient world. Yet in the Table
there is no mention of God, nor is there any mention of Israel.
Yet how different is this Table from others we possess that have
been compiled by other peoples. In the latter there is normally a
'most favoured nation' clause. In the Babylonian list, for
example, the Babylonians are at the centre of the attention of
the gods. Where you have polytheism you cannot find the concept of the oneness of man. Our chapter, on the contrary, contains material that we discover to be basic to Israel's sacred
Scripture. Clearly what it means to be the People of God is
something quite different from the pagan views of election held
in both the ancient and the modern world.

What are we to make of all this, then? In the first place Israel
is evidently unique, not because of any special position for her
in the Table of Nations, but because only she is called into
being at the Word of god, 12: 1 – 'Now the Lord *said* to
Abram, "Go" . . .'. This special calling is revealed not because
of anything that Israel is in herself. Instead it is made in order
that Israel may become God's special instrument of blessing to
all the other nations listed in the Table, 12: 3b; Isa. 49: 6. Israel
is not placed at the centre of the life of the nations, as von Rad

points out, in the way that the Chinese, for example, have always thought of themselves as being at the centre of the world, or in modern times, as certain ecclesiastics like to place their own denomination. They like to call it 'the bridge church', and thus place it at the centre. Israel, of course, is not yet in existence at the period depicted by the Table; for Israel is a people elect of faith and she is not born till Abram appears. So J and P have both resisted the temptation to throw Israel's origin back into this ancient list.

The total number of names is given as 71. The tradition to which Israel consistently held was to that there were 70 nations in the ancient world. In the old poem preserved for us in Deut. 32 we read (in the Hebrew) that there were as many nations in the world as the 70 sons of Jacob; cf. Ex. 1: 5. So it means that God had called the 70 extended families that comprise Israel into being with the express purpose of their serving the nations of the world. It has been suggested that in the course of the transmission of the text of our chapter an error has crept in. Perhaps a literal-minded scribe has entered a name on his own initiative, unaware of the theological relevance to Israel's election of the number 70. (See also Luke 10: 1.) Finally, at v. 32, we discover P's signature again as he links the Table of the Nations to the story that follows, for at 11: 1 we once again meet with the phrase, 'the whole earth'. Any critical commentary on Genesis deals with the problems attached to the individual names listed in the Table. Here we shall refer to only a few of these names.

In the first place the dependence of 1 Chron. 1 upon both Gen. 5 and 10 is noticeable. *Magog*, v. 2, appears right at the beginning of our list. In Ezek. 38 the nation of this name is known as Gog, its land as Magog. In that chapter Ezekiel declares that this people is the very incarnation of the enmity of natural man against God and against God's plan for the redemption of the world through his selection of Israel. Yet this name stands insouciantly at the head of the list of nations! And the Magog here is the son of the Japheth who survived the Flood! Thus he belonged to the forgiven generation, even as did Sodom and Gomorrah, v. 19 (see Gen. 18: 16–19: 29), cities that in the course of time became synonymous with the culture of the human being at his worst (see Deut. 29: 23; 32: 32;

Isa. 1: 9–10; 3: 9; Jer. 23: 14; 49: 18; Lam. 4: 6; Ezek. 16: 46; Amos 4: 11; Matt. 10: 15; Rom. 9: 29; 2 Peter 2: 6; Jude 7; Rev. 11: 8). These are listed quite naturally along with the other peoples of the earth.

The name *Babel*, v. 10, that is, Babylon, along with Erech and Accad (all of them 'in the land of Shinar'), follows upon mention of Nimrod; 'he was a mighty hunter before the Lord', AV, or 'he was the first on earth to be a mighty man', RSV. (Isa. 10: 5 recognizes the difficulty of such a statement.) Some scholars identify Nimrod with Sargon the Great of Akkad, 2630–2575 B.C. The figure of Nimrod clearly represents the kind of civilization referred to in 4: 17–22, where we saw how God's plan and purpose for man was to develop the arts and crafts and to rule the forces of nature. Yet it is just at this point that man's pride and insolence take over, and militate against God's plan for the good of all men. Erech and Accad were the great civilizations of Mesopotamia out of which later on God called Abram to depart, 12: 1; while the great city of Babylon came to symbolize this very gigantism of secular man. This issue is dealt with in chapter 11. For Nebuchadnezzar, in historical times, called himself 'Kings of kings and lord of lords', and was outstanding even for the ancient world for his cruelty in war. Actually the incident connected with Peleg, v. 25, 'for in his days the earth was divided', may also refer to the event recorded in chapter 11.

The name *Jaktan*, v. 25, is of importance in linking the faith of the people of the Qoran with the OT. Jaktan seems to have been the mighty progenitor of the South Arabs. The spelling of the name was later modified to *Qahtan*, a name much handled by the Muslim genealogists. He too was a descendant of Shem, the name of that human grouping to which Israel belonged. Again, the name *Hazarmaveth*, v. 26, another important name to the Muslim believer, developed, as some scholars believe, into Hadramaut. Thus such peoples as the Amalekites and other 'Arab' nations, throughout the course of history regarded as Israel's mortal enemies, Ex. 17: 8–16, etc., are listed without rancour or prejudice, and even with studied scientific objectivity, so as to possess one heritage as fellow Semites with Israel.

At v. 21 the name *Eber* occurs. From it the name *'ibhri* probably derives. In English, *'ibhri* is read as Hebrew. This does not mean, however, that it is the Israelites who are referred to here. *'ibhri* was the name given in the Near East to all kinds of nomadic peoples, for the word simply means 'nomad'. Waves of such came into Syria–Palestine 1500–1200 B.C. One group of these thereupon created the state of Aram. When Israel was in Egypt, Moses' people received the name *Apiriu*, but so did others who had wandered out of the desert into the cultivated and well-watered Nile basin, Ex. 2: 16; 3: 18; 5: 3. The name appears on the stele of Pharaoh Seti I (1300 B.C.) at Beth Shean in southern Galilee. And it occurs as *Habiru* on the Tell el Amarna tablets. So we are not to suppose that this name Eber necessarily fixes Israel in the Table of Nations, even though Abraham is later called *ha-'ibhri, the* Hebrew *par excellence*, 14: 13.

In the following verse, v. 22, *Arpachshad* means 'the territory of the Chasd', or the Chaldeans. Yet neither does that fact make Israel a special case in the sight of God. We recall that Abraham came from Ur of the Chaldeans. Arpachshad is just one name in a list. In fact, its occurrence actually underlines the anomaly that Abraham was not a Jew but a Mesopotamian, a name of mere geographical significance meaning just 'Between the Rivers'!

Chapter 11

THE TOWER OF BABEL

1–9   The first part of this chapter tells of 'The Tower of Babel' though it was the walls rather than the tower of Babylon that were accounted one of the wonders of the seven wonders of the ancient world.

In one of King Nebuchadnezzar's records, 604–562 B.C., we read: 'The peoples of many nations I compelled to work on building *Etemenanki*. On its top I set up the high dwelling of lord Marduk.' This was known as 'the house of the foundation of heaven and earth'. The so-called *Esagil* tablet, dated 229 B.C., gives the exact dimensions of this 'tower'. Floor by floor, these are the measurements from the ground up:

First floor:	295′ × 295′ ×	108′	high
Second floor:	256′ × 256′ ×	59′	,,
Third floor:	197′ × 197′ ×	20′	,,
Fourth floor:	167′ × 167′ ×	20′	,,
Fifth floor:	138′ × 138′ ×	20′	,,
Sixth floor:	108′ × 108′ ×	20′	,,
Seventh floor:	79′ × 79′ ×	49′	,,

On the seventh floor stood the temple, known as *Shaharu*. This is evidently a semitic word that could mean 'sunrise'. So the tower was a kind of mountain-top. Herodotus of Halicarnassus visited this edifice in 460 B.C. 'A spiral staircase runs round it outside', he wrote. 'Half way up there are seats for resting. In the Temple there is a rich bed and a golden table, but no representation of a god. A woman spends the night there; she is designated by the god himself.' It seems that the god was supposed to sleep on the bed with the woman, and then to descend and enter a magnificent temple situated at ground level. Is Gen. 6: 1–4 an echo of such a belief?

The above is, of course, a description of a ziggurat. The building of such towers goes back right as far as the fourth millenium B.C., a great renewal of energy manifesting itself in the twenty-second and twenty-first centuries, that is to say, about 300 years before the date we usually assign to Abraham. Several of these structures were certainly standing in Abraham's day. Ezekiel and Deutero-Isaiah would in their turn visit Nebuchadnezzar's 'tower', for it was demolished only in 478 B.C. by Xerxes, king of Persia. Today its site is only an enormous hole filled with water.

Others tell how each of the levels of an ancient ziggurat was painted a different colour, each the traditional colour of one of the seven planets visible to the naked eye. The archaeologist Parrot, in the year 1932, excavated the bases of several of these mighty buildings, and found that they were composed of baked brick, whose courses were joined with bitumen, 11: 3, and which in our day are still so solid that they resisted his workmen's picks.

Scholars are divided on the purpose of the Mesopotamian ziggurat. Some suggest that it was the throne of the god, even as was Mount Olympus in Greece. Others that the seven levels were symbolic of the heavens with their seven planets. Others suppose that the ziggurat was the tomb of a king. The majority view, however, is that the tower held up the temple of the god, ready for the latter to 'come down' (cf. 11: 5) onto it from heaven. For the top storey was sometimes called a 'house', the place where god and man could meet. Thus the ziggurat, in this majority view, represented what almost all nations have thought about the meaning and significance of religion as such, in that religion is the name given to the struggling ascent by man as he seeks to reach up to the divine, and only thereafter to the descent of the divine to man. That is to say, the ascent of man comes first. For man has always taken it for granted that he can 'build the kingdom', produce the perfect society, 'make a name for himself', 11: 4, and so on. Only after he has begun to do so does the god assume any importance at all, so as to become (as we say today) merely 'the god of the gaps'. All that man seems to want of god is a reassurance from him that man can 'do it alone' – that is why he seeks merely the divine seal upon the civilization which he has already created and then only in order that it might last for ever. 'United in one culture, they only want god to absolutize their creation as final', to use the words of one German commentator. Thus the votive offerings

made by worshippers of statuettes of figures with clasped hands
found at the foot of some of the ziggurats will have been placed
there with the purpose of begging the god to maintain the culture that man had already produced.

Such then is the historical background of our story. Our
interest, however, is to discover what those theological insights
are which J has to offer us when he uses the factual nature of the
historical ziggurat as he brings to completion his section of
Gen. 1–11.

1 J begins with a phrase which in English is almost equal
to 'Once upon a time', NEB. Clearly he is declaring that he is
telling us a tale, one that is to be understood in terms of parable
or allegory. In this theological tale, then, he says that in the
early days of man all the peoples of the earth understood each
other; they possessed, he says, only a limited vocabulary, for
they had little to say to one another. J does *not* mean that all
men agreed with each other. In fact they all uttered the same
sounds when angry, all knew when the other was threatening,
and so on. The proper *historical* statement, on the other hand,
has already been made at 10: 5, 20, 31.

2 The next three verbs have no subject, for J is not want-
ing to spoil his tale with the use of unknown names. It is *man*
who migrates from the depths of Asia, man made in the image
of God; it is man who then reaches in his travels what to the
folk of those days was self-evidently the centre of the world, the
Tigris–Euphrates Plain. J knew that in his day there were traces
of civilization on it going back over countless centuries.

3 Man is a co-operative being. The new settlers discuss
their plan of action and agree. To the east of the mountains of
Ararat men had built their civilization with the use of stone.
Shinar, however, is an alluvial plain. So man has now to learn
new skills and new techniques. So 'they' manufacture bricks
from mud and use bitumen to bind the bricks together.

4 Man's inventiveness and willingness to co-operate
excites him to build on the Plain not mere hovels but a city,
with streets, houses, public buildings, walls, and, most importantly, in its midst a tower that, to the ancient world, could
be described almost as a sky-scraper. The Israelites did, in fact,
in their migration to Canaan, meet with cities 'fortified up to
heaven', Deut. 1: 28; 9: 1. Isaiah regarded such fortifications

and towers as marks of human defiance against God, Isa. 13: 19; 14: 13. For the building of such walls and of such a tower was, of course, a religious act. There was no such concept in the ancient world as what we know as secularism, the belief that there is nothing in human life except matter, or that man lives by bread alone. For in his heart man knows that he is showing arrogance and defiance against the divinity; for, as we read, man said to himself, 'lest we be scattered . . .'. J shows that man's conscience has told him that he had no business to do what he was doing, and that it was self-interest which was overruling his conscience. That unity is strength is what even early man knew well. Yet his religiousness now misleads him, for his faith has been put in the wrong place. We read that man planned *first* to build a city. Only *then* did he think of anchoring it to the sky. That is to say, man sets out to insult God by seeking, not for fellowship with him nor obedience to him, but merely for a religious sanction to suit his own convenience for what he has already built. Man insolently hopes to find unity by *using* the divinity for his own ends. So he exhibits the stupidity of Cain who built a city in the land of Wandering, 4: 16–17.

This approach to religion has been endemic in all human cultures. There is the East Asian parable of the mountain with its top reaching to the abode of the Divine Being. In the parable all religious paths lead up to the same point on the summit of the mountain. All religions, it is implied, are equally good. All of them *elevate* man into the presence of God so that once there man discovers that he is really one over all the earth and speaks the one language of faith.

But the biblical revelation gives short shrift to this eastern parable. Man cannot climb up to God, the Bible declares. Man cannot find unity by by-passing the profound problems of life, pain, suffering, greed, selfishness, and death itself, as, for example, the Marxist seeks to do. Even the modern 'spiritually minded' person who is ever seeking new religious experiences is by-passing reality when he ignores the dirt of the market-place. We have already learned that greed and selfishness actually separate man from man. But more, as we are now to see, they separate man from God. On the other hand, God is utterly 'above' all man's self-centred striving after unity and attempts to make a 'name' for himself as a spiritual giant. For it is God alone who can make a 'name' for himself, as the whole OT declares, Isa. 63: 12; Jer. 32: 20; Neh. 9: 10.

5   'And the Lord came down.' It was not *Elohim* who did so. J had refrained from making any identification of the Divine Being at the beginning of his tale, for the god might equally have been Marduk or Baal. But now, without beating about the bush, he declares flatly that YHWH came down, Yahweh the God of the Covenant, the God of revelation, the God who said to Moses. 'I have come down into the horror of the slavery of my people in Egypt . . .', Ex. 3: 7, the Yahweh who did so for the loving, creative, saving purpose which we have discovered is the mark of Israel's God, the God of the incarnational and redemptive process.

We should note the touch of humour here, and compare it with Ps. 2: 4. No matter how high man hopes to be able to climb up to God, God must still come down to man. Moreover, he comes down only when *he* determines that the time is ripe to do so, Gen. 18: 21; 28: 17; Ex. 19: 20; John 1: 14. The biblical faith is thus not to be described in terms of 'religion' at all, as we have kept reiterating. Rather it is to be regarded as revelation, for, from Genesis onwards, it records the 'coming down' at historical moments of God to man, and each time it happens, it occurs without any co-operation by man. All man has to do is obey. Thus it is that man's unity can be created by God alone. For God is utterly above man's puny designs and philosophies. Insignificant man can only plan and work for his own success and happiness. But in face of that God shows his grace by preventing man from making things even worse than they have worked out to be. For this reason YHWH comes down 'to see the city and the tower which the *sons of men* [clearly in contrast to the phrase *sons of God*, 6: 2] had built'.

6   God takes man's search for a false, man-made unity seriously, a unity, as we have said, that ignores the facts of life. Such a unity would soon dissolve, being based merely on economic and political factors, and so is quite superficial. 'The city and the tower' may here speak of the same thing, in that the phrase forms a hendiadys. That is to say, the city, which ought to be the mark of a healthy civilization, was itself the tower of man's arrogance and pride. We note with interest that there is no mention ever in the book of Exodus of the great pyramids of

Gizeh. The pyramids that we travel to Egypt to gaze at today had been standing there over a thousand years before Moses was even born. Clearly God's concern is not with man's technological civilization, but with man himself. For technology by itself does not build the Kingdom of God. J understood this matter even in days of long ago and because of this was able to express the mind of God upon it in this basic piece of theological writing. A good translation of what God says here might be: 'Actually nothing is inaccessible to them'. This is what we have already discovered at 3: 22.

7–9 And so the corporate Divine Personality, who can talk to himself within himself, cf. 1: 26; 3: 22, using (at v. 4) language parallel with that of corporate man made in his image, makes the decision to 'come down' to prevent that very thing from happening – the unification of man on the wrong basis. And this *for man's own good*. Deut. 8: 17. Yet to our human understanding God now does a strange thing. He actually allows sin to work for him! Remembering that sin separates man from man, God here allows to take place the reverse of the hope which man had expressed at 11: 3–4 about the motivation of his basic intentions. What happens is that God does not destroy the city from without; he lets it destroy itself from within.

To this end God, once again, does not do what we might expect him to do. If he had been Zeus of the Greeks he would have hurled a thunderbolt against the city and the tower, as Jesus' disciples expected God to do in their day, Luke 9: 54. But God knows man would not see any such visible judgment upon his insolence as valid at all. Instead of the thunderbolt, therefore, God uses the natural process of the break-up and subdividing of man's natural groupings and languages to the point where unity is no longer conceivable; and so communication between the groups becomes no longer possible. Because this very thing now happens, man has necessarily to leave off building his all-powerful unified empire. The Hebrew in this sentence can mean that God 'made their speech sound foolish' to each other. The result was that they scattered in all directions as if God had just said 'Poof!'

It seems from many instances in the OT that the Israelite ear enjoyed listening to assonance in speech, in the juxtaposition of two or more words that sounded alike. It seems that people even supposed that there was a similarity of meaning between two words just because they sounded alike. The word translated 'confused' is *balal*. But it sounds (the Hebrews supposed) like Babel. The latter is the Hebrew spelling of the city we know as Babylon.

Babylon was a big city. Conquered peoples of many tongues lived in and around it at all periods of its long existence. This was true of it when Israel too was exiled there in the sixth century B.C. Then she must have met with a veritable babble of tongues. But our chapter here is not discussing the historical Babylon; it is concerned rather with the idea of *babel*. The book of Deuteronomy in contrast constantly insists that Israel will find unity at that spot where God had put *his* Name with the end in view that in his good time all men might be united as one through worshipping him, Isa. 2: 1–4; Eph. 1: 10. This follows from what we read later in Gen. 12, where Prologue moves into History. There God says to Abram, 'I will make *your* name great, and you will be a blessing to all men' – the obverse of the story discussed here.

But Babel really means 'Gate of God'. In his *Cosmos and History*, 1954, pp. 12 ff., Mircea Eliade writes: 'The pinnacle of the ziggurat was the meeting point of heaven and earth, or, in Babylonian, "The Gate of the Apsu" [the Abyss]'. But now God has undone all that. The Gate of God has now become the source of confusion, the obverse of the false unity that man had thought he had created as his own good idea. Evidently man has always to keep on learning that his idea of asking the divine to confirm as right his own selfish plans can only appear sadly comical in the eyes of God. We might even go so far as to say that this story is a condemnation of the religions and philosophies of man (cf. 1 Cor. 1: 25). We might even go further and agree with the famous saying of Karl Marx, when he declared that religion is the opiate of the people.

From Pictorial Theology to Historical Theology

10   This verse picks up from chapter 5. It gives us the genealogy of a second group of ten persons descending from Shem, so that, ending with Abram, it makes the latter the twentieth generation of mankind. Chapter 10 has already listed the descendants of Ham and Japheth. Now P continues

with the line that descends through *Arpachshad*. The whole list
forms a series of names that glide from the area of theological
picture language, beginning with Seth at 4: 26, the 'father' of
believing man, viz. Enosh, into that of history. It thus forms the
link between the biblical Prologue (Gen. 1–11) and the beginning of the story of God's redemptive purpose in history. With
Gen. 12, therefore, we enter the historical situation of the Near
East at the Middle Bronze Age, 1800–1500 B.C.

26   We pass down the list to the name *Terah*. Here P's
toledoth ('These are the generations') climax in a trio of names,
Terah's three sons, Abram, Nahor, and Haran. These all lived
in the city of Ur of the Chaldeans. The name Chaldeans ceased
to be used about 1500 B.C. Thereafter the name Kasdim took its
place. The city of Ur in those days was a great seaport. Today
its ruins are far inland; for since Abram's day the Tigris and
Euphrates rivers have built up a large delta at their common
mouth. Ur was excavated in the 1920s by the archaeologist
Woolley who uncovered the remains of a cultured society going
back to 4000 B.C. What is of special interest to us is that the
wharves of the city accommodated ships that traded as far
away from Ur as the great land of India. Here then the 'wisdom
of the east' met with the culture of Mesopotamia to form the
matrix of the new movement in God's plan when 'the Lord
said to Abram, "Go forth" ' on that journey which transformed
the world, 12: 1.

27–29   Terah means 'moon'. It can therefore be supposed
that Abram's father was a moon-worshipper. The name Abram
probably means 'My Father (God) is exalted'; and Sarai means
'princess'. Haran is a place name; but a man could and did call
himself after a place. Lot is mentioned, for he plays a significant
part in the later story as the necessary foil against which God's
grace is revealed, chapters 13 and 19. What differentiates both
the Prologue and the History that begins at chapter 12 from all
other human documents of ancient times is that these two sections of Genesis take a realistic view both of the sinfulness of
man, cf. 6: 5, and of the grace of God. They form a true background to what Paul says at Rom. 5: 20: 'Where sin increased,
grace abounded all the more'.

31   One did not travel directly from Ur to Canaan, for
between them there lies bleak desert. The traveller goes in a

half-circle, following the so-called Fertile Crescent. So this extended family now finds itself at the half-way point to Canaan and in the town of Haran in north-west Mesopotamia. And there they stayed. Haran, like Ur, was also the converging point of many caravan routes. Numerous cultures, even that which is known later as that of the Greeks, met and mingled there, and undoubtedly these fertilized each the other. Both the time and the place were 'ripe', it would seem, for the incursion of the redemptive Word of God.

32   Finally, the last verse of the Genesis Prologue offers a figure for Terah's length of life that nicely rounds off the past and leads also to turning our eyes to the future. The fact that the date of Terah's death falls sixty years after Abram's departure from Haran is of no consequence to the writer, for he is absorbed with the reality of something that he believes to be of vastly greater significance. The little thing of vast significance is noted as if by a mere aside at v. 30: 'Now Sarai was barren; she had no child'; cf. Luke 1: 34, 37.

These few words reveal, as hardly anything else could have done, the nature of what we are reading, viz. Holy Scripture. Up to this point the Prologue has declared that the humanity whom God had made in his own image, had, by its own free will, rebelled against the divine blessing; and that even after the judgment and the renewal man had ended up in a babel of division and hopelessness. Yet it is out of this very Babel and failure of the natural processes that God's elective purpose now emerges. He chooses a woman who cannot have a baby to fulfil the promise that we are to read of in the next chapter. We, the reader, with our hindsight, know the story which chapter 12 records. We know already that Abram will become Abraham, and will be the father of the People of God and the one man through whom all the nations of the earth will be blessed. We already know that the Covenant which God made first with Abraham, and then repeated with Isaac and then Jacob, and then with the whole people of Israel, is God's method of procedure as he sets about rescuing from their hopeless state of sin the mankind who has rebelled against him. We already know that the faith and obedience of Abram, which was pictured in Noah who walked with God, turned Abram into a wanderer. We know that he does *not* try to build a city in which there is a tower with steps *up to* God, and that in fact he looks for a city that has *foundations*, whose builder and maker is God, Heb. 11: 10. Yet how could all these events have ever taken place if Sarai, as we are told here, was barren?

Evidently it is just such a *contretemps* that God chooses to use to help us learn that 'my Kingdom is not of this world'. God's Kingdom does not evolve by natural processes. It advances by crises of faith. Evidently the People of God are not called into being just to become a nation like other nations. God's Kingdom grows by the power of the Word. The Word performs God's elective purpose, when he chooses one man and passes by another man, chooses a barren woman and passes by a woman with child. The Word did not sound in Terah's heart, nor in that of Abram's brothers. It was Abram alone to whom the Word was addressed, that Word whose reality we recognized at 1: 3, the Word of creation, and therefore also of re-creation.

So a baby is born from a barren womb; life, so to speak, actually comes out of death, even Light is born out of chaos, 1: 3. Such strange things can happen only because God has entered into history *in* his Word. He 'comes down' and clothes himself with human history so that man's sinful plans and rebellious nature, as he seeks to build his cities and towers up to God in the land of Nod, actually become the medium that God chooses to use. For in and through these plans, in fact even *out of* them, there is born the Kingdom of God. We read that Noah *did*, 6: 22, what God commanded him. The theological story now becomes history at 12: 4, where we read that 'Abram *went*, as the Lord had *told* him'.

It is thus the twentieth generation of mankind that, in obeying the Word, becomes God's ally when he initiates his plan for the salvation of the world. Yet what God had said to Abram was, 'Through your *descendants* you will be a blessing, and all the families of the earth shall be blessed'. 'Now Sarai was barren; she had no child . . .'.